Dear Chris

Dear Chris

Conversations with My Son

Valerie Bell-Smith

To order additional copies of this book, contact:
Xlibris Corporation
1-888-795-4274
www.Xlibris.com
Orders@Xlibris.com
66194

CONTENTS

Conclusion

FOR

CHRISTOPHER JERMAINE SMITH

Let us pray.

Lord, please place Your spirit into these pages with a little bit of Elgin's and

Christopher's too.

Bless every reader. Allow them to see less of me and all of You.

Guide their hearts and thoughts beyond the suffering and pain.

Cause them to look past my often selfish whining

and the times that I complained.

Open up their hearts to receive inspiration, encouragement, and renewed faith.

Remind them to trust You in their own walk toward Your greater mercy and grace.

To You be the glory.

Amen.

Acknowledgments

I thank my husband, Elgin, and our boys, Christopher, Jeremy, and Joshua, for their love, support, and patience as we have struggled. Thank you to our parents and sisters for never giving up on us and always being just a prayer and phone call away. I really appreciate all my friends and colleagues who just stepped into our lives and went to work helping in so many ways. May God continue to bless all of us!

Preface

AML—acute myelogenous leukemia? Okay, are you serious? I mean, what is this anyway? How dare this disease interrupt our lives? Why us? Why now? Questions often go unanswered. You can search and find many probable answers, often digging deeply and uncovering truths that are difficult to grab on to. So if you can't find the source of the struggle, you then seek to assign some meaning to it all. At some point, you stop and take a look around you, and then you realize that your initial questions may need to be rephrased—Why not us? Why not now?

I am so blessed to share this story of faith, healing, and grace of my family. I had a marriage of eighteen years to my late husband, Elgin. We shared a total of twenty-two years together. I know it may sound corny, but when I first saw him, time literally stood still. I will never forget that moment. I was on a break at my after-school job, enjoying my favorite chocolate chip ice-cream cone. A handsome tall guy with dimples got out of a cute little Volkswagen Bug. He appeared to glide across the parking lot in slow motion. I felt a warmness engulf me; my vision became blurred. I quickly shook it off and surmised that I must have experienced a brain freeze or something. After all, I'd seen that cute little car several times and wondered whom it belonged to. The guy in the cute little Bug would later reveal to my coworker (whom he knew from their high school) that he had "noticed" me too. He later started coming through my line at the supermarket. I agreed to dinner and a movie, and the rest is history!

We would later commit to spending our lives together and be blessed with three wonderful sons: Christopher, twenty; Jeremy, aged seventeen; and Joshua, aged thirteen. Our boys, like all children, are wonderful, amazing blessings. Each with their own individual personalities that remind us of who we are and our impact on their lives. Joshua, our youngest son, is very inquisitive, full of energy, an artist, a musician, and actor. He also loves sports. Our middle son, Jeremy, is quiet and mild mannered. Although he is not my biological son, I love him because he is so much a part of his father. To look at him is like seeing pictures from my husband's childhood come to life. Jeremy has been a distant part of our lives but also a new blessing. He has become a new source of light.

And then there's our Christopher. Our firstborn and the owner of a large part of my heart. When he was born, he weighed almost ten pounds! The nurses called him the football player in the nursery because he was almost too big for his bassinet. Shortly after I held him for the first time, they took him away, and when I saw him again, they had inserted an IV into his head. Being the young mother that I was, I didn't question it—I was just angry they had shaved my newborn baby's hair. They said something about his oxygen levels but later decided he was fine and sent him home. Two years later, he was diagnosed with asthma, which would start a lifetime of IVs, doctor's visits, albuterol inhaler pumps, and oxygen treatments. Looking back on it all now, I am racking my brain trying to figure out if there are correlations with the outcome of the impending leukemia that ultimately took his life.

For the past few years, both my husband (Elgin) and our oldest son (Christopher) were embattled with cancer: Elgin since 1997 and Christopher since 2005. My husband originally had testicular cancer in 1997. Four years after, he was cancer free, and then it reoccurred in September 2006 while our oldest son was undergoing treatment for leukemia, which was officially diagnosed in February 2006. When Christopher was initially diagnosed, he was a freshman at Georgia Southern University (GSU). He was transported by ambulance back home to Atlanta, where he underwent several months of chemotherapy treatment and then later returned to school at GSU. However, the leukemia eventually returned. So he was forced to return home to Atlanta to resume treatment. This time, treatment would include radiation and possibly a bone marrow transplant. When he came back home the last time, he and his father were both in the hospital. Things became quite hard for us financially, spiritually, and emotionally. I thought I was going to lose my mind! It seemed as if every day presented some new challenge. When one was well, the other was sick and vice versa. Our youngest son, Joshua, went through his own struggles seeing his father and older brother, who are his mentors and heroes, going through so much. He witnessed their hair loss, extreme weight loss, pain, nausea, etc. Joshua tends to internalize his feelings, but he was visibly saddened, confused, and very angry. He tried to be the "man" of the house helping with chores, etc. In my attempts to be the rock for all my "men," I would put up my own front of strength in their presence, but suffered my own silent struggle behind closed doors. I would cry myself to sleep, find myself crying in my car. If someone called and said hello, I would cry. Each day just blended into the next. There were times when I couldn't separate the darkness from the light. I had no shoulder to cry on. I was used to leaning on my husband when I was tired, confused, lonely, or uncertain. My oldest son was like my brother. He was my best friend. I was accustomed to him brushing my hair and massaging away the stress in my neck from a long day at work. He always kept me smiling with his wit and humor. Yet it was in these moments of loneliness and despair when I began to truly experience God. I felt His presence and heard His voice deep within myself giving me the courage and the strength to get up and keep moving.

I was completely responsible for their physical care which included everything associated with caring for them, providing transportation to countless medical appointments, and administering various medications. My job had been our sole source of income, so I also attempted to start a small business for extra money. When a major illness strikes, medical expenses skyrocket, and there's not much available in terms of assistance unless you meet certain income levels—which we did not. I would later find out that there were organizations that might have provided assistance, but when you're in the eye of a storm, it's hard to focus on anything other than what is in front of you. All my mental, physical, and emotional energy was exhausted just dealing with daily life and a longing for normalcy. For me, there was hardly the time or patience for researching financial aid, etc. Prior to my husband becoming ill, he had started a new job but had not worked long enough to receive sick leave or any other benefits. Thankfully, both Elgin and Christopher were covered under my insurance. We had to make certain that Christopher remained in school; otherwise, he would not be covered at all. I was often afraid he might not be able to return to school because of the illness and would then have no medical coverage at all.

For a while, both Elgin and Chris began to experience restored health. Chris was blessed to be accepted into Morehouse College, his initial school of choice. Now he could attend school closer to home. We began to trust God to make a way for tuition, books, etc. He worked on his studies until he was no longer able to write and see clearly.

Prior to either of them becoming ill, due to a downsizing, Elgin lost his job, and we lost our house. We didn't have a financial plan or any type of safety net. Christopher had recently started college, without any scholarships, only student loans (which don't cover all expenses). So any savings we had were already gone. We had to move to a small apartment (this entire situation presented its own challenges). We began 2006 with the loss of our home and our oldest son being ill. He was away at college at the time and had not been formally diagnosed for the symptoms he was experiencing. Shortly after, cancer reoccurred in my husband, which ensued with more challenges than I care to revisit.

We have since been blessed with a beautiful new house. Elgin was recovering from a vigorous round of chemotherapy the night we closed on the house. It was always our goal to give our boys the best. We were not going to let these illnesses keep us from having the home we so deserved. Yes, the enemy has attempted to put my thoughts over into doubt and fear, but I am quickly reminded of the journey that God has brought us through. I am reminded of how he carried us when we were too tired or simply unable to walk ourselves. Today, I have a renewed mind and spirit of peace. I trust Him fully.

The heartache and pain expressed in these pages are often pleasantly interrupted with instances of joy and encouragement. Perhaps most prominent is the presence of faith. I never lost hope. Hope breeds faith, and faith pleases God. This entire experience has allowed me to develop a closer relationship with Him. I understand that I am a reflection of His glory. Our struggles are circumstantial to the overall life experience. The response to any struggle starts and finishes with faith. He has a plan; there are great things ahead. The journey continues to unfold. To God be the glory!

Someone asked a question, why do we sing?
When we lift our hands to Jesus what do we really mean?

INTRODUCTION

Chapter 1

In My Son's Words

In his determination to continue his studies and maintain his scholarships, Chris wrote the following essay to the Georgia HOPE Scholarship Committee:

For over a week I had been experiencing a pain that was all together excruciating in my legs, arms, and ankles. Neither the painkillers that were prescribed to me nor the rest that I forced myself to seek did anything to alleviate the pain. I would dare say that both—if anything—served to exacerbate my distress; so, after over a week of brushing aside the pain, ignoring my discomfort, and willing myself to meander through my daily routine, I dropped my pride and what machismo I could muster, and checked myself into the East Georgia Regional Medical Center in Statesboro, GA. Once at East Georgia Regional, I was humbled as I had to grapple with the fear of not knowing. See, I didn't know what was wrong, how serious my health issue was, or what the pain portended. The fact that the doctors did not present me with anything conclusive in addition to the series of tests to which I was subjected did nothing to allay my fears. It is always easier to deal with fear when there is something on which to center one's fear. Not knowing forces anyone to admit a total lack of control and vulnerability.

I concluded that my condition was serious when the doctors agreed that it was best that I be sent to Northside Hospital in Atlanta, GA, to receive the diagnosis that had eluded me there. Three days later, I received the diagnosis—Leukemia. Wow! I, who am never at a loss for words found myself . . . speechless. This diagnosis meant that I had to withdraw from my courses and return home to Atlanta indefinitely. What plans I had were now placed on hold; what goals, dreams and aspirations I envisioned were now shelved. I find it funny that when referencing anyone's graduation this question ultimately arises: "So, when do you plan to walk?" I also find humor in the fact that the leukemia manifested itself through pain in my legs. Thus,

19

my walk—in a complete sense, physically, educationally, emotionally, and spiritually—was incomprehensively affected.

I am not exaggerating; I, Christopher Jermaine Smith, had meticulously planned the details of my undergraduate experience. Each educational experience I had made was a link in a concentrated chain of events which were designed to culminate in my career as a corporate lawyer. I was the designer, but somewhere along the line, one of the links of the chain broke, which does not say much for my designing skills. Honestly, I was not prepared for the increased pain, the nausea, vomiting, fatigue, and the endless supply of medication, the debilitating procedures—chemotherapy, bone marrow biopsies, and blood transfusions; but here, "on the other side of through," with the Leukemia in remission, the whole experience enriched me.

Why do I say this experience enriched me? It gave me a more profound perspective on everything. But most importantly, it forced me to reevaluate my priorities, reconsider all my relationships, and reconstruct the same. All this is important but I choose to focus on my future. A few short weeks ago, I was terrified that I would have no future to consider, but through it all I held fast to my hope. What is hope? It is but a focus and an attitude. Focus implies direction and attitude implies spirit. Hope is spirited direction. Notice that neither component extinguishes or undermines the other, rather they enhance one another. I am now, after and in light of everything, wholly driven and determined to continue my education. My hope(s) hinged on "HOPE," the scholarship that is. I am completely convinced that I did not undergo all this to simply rest on my laurels. I endured everything that I mentioned, because it was meant for me to, as I also know that it was also meant for me to survive.

Carpe diem!!! This saying has new meaning for me. Each morning I wake, I am determined to seize the day. It is hope that allows me to say and do this.

Chapter 2

What's in a Name?

What's in a name? When we name our children, it's for various reasons. Perhaps we want to honor a loved one; maybe the name just sounds cute, or it just seems to "fit." Perhaps all are true for your baby brother Joshua. One night, just before he was born, I dreamt that a baby boy was peeking around the corner of my dresser and smiling at me. From that day on, I started calling him Joshua. As he has grown older, I've gone on to call him Josh, Joshy, Cutie Pie, and Cheeky Bear, among many other little mommy-only names.

Josh is my little trooper. When Chris initially became ill, Josh was a bit scared and concerned. He had Elgin around to keep him preoccupied, so they would and hang out when Chris couldn't. He and Elgin were always very close. Then when Elgin also became ill, it really hit Josh hard.

Let's consider our other son Jeremy. I am surmising that his name comes from the prophet Jeremiah. When our journey with leukemia began, I was given a scripture from a complete stranger. A woman I'd never seen just walked up to me and handed it to me on a piece of paper, Jeremiah 29:11, which includes a verse that says, "I know the plans I have for you." This was truly the Holy Spirit, and it took me two years to understand this occurrence. This Holy Spirit, which is with us to give us comfort, will allow instances to happen without immediate reason, and as it has been said, "We'll understand it better by and by."

And then there is my Christopher, which means "of Christ." His name has further been defined as Christopheros, "carrier of the light"! When I first met Chris, I knew he was of Christ. What mother could ever forget the first time they held their first child? I will never forget. He was a beautiful nine pound, five ounces of joy. In fact, he was the biggest baby born in the nursery the night of April 16, 1987. I was so young and naive. The nine-month eternity had all of a sudden melted into moments, and there he was in my arms. His eyes were wide open and pierced straight to my soul. Though he had barely uttered a whimper, he spoke to me with such volume. I was frightened but compelled to be the best mother I could be.

For the first time in my life, I truly felt my heart opened and filled with love. Certainly, I'd loved before, my parents, my sister, and of course, my husband, Elgin. But my dear Chris, wow! What God intended for love to be had somehow consumed me with the presence of my son. Chris introduced me to life, womanhood, motherhood, and a strength within that I never knew I had.

I pray that Chris will forever know that I love him so very deeply, and despite our struggles and the terrible effects of cancer, nothing could ever separate my heart from my baby.

Since he has been gone, we were blessed with a godson who bears his name. I have carefully explained its origin to his mother, and I am waiting with anticipation to someday share with him the same.

Chapter 3

I Miss You

December 9, 2009

Dear Chris,

I miss you so much, Chris. When I started writing these letters to you, my original intentions were mixed. I was agitated with you because you often frustrated me when I would attempt to tell you something for your own good. I was so young when you were born; I always treated you more like my best friend than my son. We were best friends for so long that when I tried to be "Mom," you would simply ask me if I was trying to "play the mommy role." And then there were so many times that you would become philosophical and justify yourself. You wouldn't allow me to get my point across, and we would find ourselves in a debate. Debating was one of your strong points and not so much for me. You were always an independent thinker, strong willed and determined. Once you had your mind made up about something, that was it. The only way I could get you to give in was if I pouted. You couldn't resist giving in to my girlish whimpers. Nonetheless, you had this habit of further agitating me by telling me you did not enjoy reading. For so long, we would "debate" about you reading. Guess what, I know you were very well-read—there is no way you could have been so witty and filled with so much knowledge otherwise. I know you would read while I wasn't paying attention. So this letter was also my attempt to gain the satisfaction of not only forcing you to consider my point of view, but also to actually see you reading! Since you would always win at our little debates, I started writing down my points and thoughts for you to consider once you read these letters.

I can be honest now. For so long, you were my source of strength, courage, and motivation. You brought true meaning to my life. I have never wanted to accomplish any great feat in my life, like saving the world. But I always knew that I wanted to leave my impression, a mark that would forever tell the world that I was here. When you were born, you became that mark. Before I met you, I had always thought that my mark would be made through music. I would dream of becoming a famous entertainer. Fortune and fame would make my name known throughout the world! For so long,

23

I dwelled in this focus, which had no true meaning or value. It was all just a dream. Then you came into my life, and you became my audience and my number one fan. You accepted my voice and began to empower me.

Upon facing this terrible illness, I would briefly find myself wondering how I could possibly face life without you. Every decision I have made, every moment since I first laid eyes on you, I have known that I had to take care of myself so I could work hard and take care of you. Being a mother is the greatest joy and pain imaginable. I will never forget the first time I held you. I can still feel the bundle of warmth that existed in my arms. Our eyes locked, and we were instantly spiritually connected. As you got older, we grew so attached to each other. I shared almost everything with you: my hopes, dreams, and aspirations. You would always listen in sweet silence. You developed a special sense for me, and you could tell whether I was happy or sad or just needed a hug. I can recall several instances where our thoughts were so in tune that we could feel each other even when we were miles apart. When you went away to college, we would find ourselves calling one another at the exact same time.

Once I began writing these letters, I just couldn't stop long enough to give them to you. There was always one distraction or another. I wrote almost daily over the course of this journey. All my letters are not included here, just enough to share our story. These letters are only a glimpse of our experience with life and cancer. The focus is not really on the illness but more on the emotional, spiritual, mental, and financial struggles that still keep me constantly on bended knees. I pray that our story will help someone in their own struggle, *whatever* it may be, to keep up the good fight of faith. Our story is one of struggle and triumph that I pray will encourage others, provide cancer awareness and the importance of keeping God first, appreciate meaningful relationships, and live the best life right now!

Someone may be wondering, When we sing our song
At times we may be crying, and nothing's even wrong.

2006

Chapter 4

Mr. Wonderful

February 18, 2006

Dear Chris,

I t was a cold December day when you called home from school to say hello. You had taken an exam and felt pretty confident about your performance, but the answer sheet was blurry. Lately, things were getting blurry in both your eyes. We laughed at the possibility of you having to wear glasses. This was one of many conversations we had lately that included concerns about your eyes, so I insisted you come home for an eye exam. The doctor at the eye clinic appeared to be quite concerned and immediately referred us to a specialist at Piedmont Hospital, where it was determined there was some optic nerve swelling in both eyes. We were instructed to visit another specialist—three doctors in one day! This one was even more concerned and hurriedly sent us to yet another specialist—four doctors in one day! This one determined that you were suffering from sarcoidosis, an inflammation of the nerve tissue. He prescribed a seven-day steroid treatment, which worked quite well. And although you missed a couple of exams, you, in your determination, returned to school.

A few days later, you began calling home with complaints of pain in your legs, ankles, and arms. Since you had started a weight training class, we figured you probably pulled something and should take an over-the-counter pain medicine. I later found out you were literally eating pain medicine! You would call almost in tears with excruciating pain. I insisted that you go to the local emergency room. After three trips to the ER, you were admitted to the hospital, and we were on our way to Statesboro to bring you home.

We stayed there with you for almost a week as the doctors with their limited resources went from a diagnosis of sickle-cell anemia to possible leukemia. We then insisted that you be formally diagnosed and treated in Atlanta. The doctors concurred, and you were transported by ambulance to Northside Hospital in Atlanta. It was there that we would meet with an oncologist. Only a couple of other times in my life had time stood still, and my vision blurred as this strange warmth cloaked my body. I knew then that this would be a life-changing experience. We seemed to glide effortlessly through corridors with signs that read Oncology, Bone Marrow, etc. Why were we there?

After several tests and conversations with doctors and nurses, who I would later come to know on a first-name basis, there was the lead oncologist assigned to you. The conclusions had been made, and the entire family was gathered around you as you lay in that hospital bed. And then there were those words: "Chris has leukemia." The doctor went on for what seemed like hours explaining the diagnosis and treatment plan, giving different scenarios, etc. His voice became like an echo, and my mind drifted away, for all I heard was that my baby had cancer.

The doctor left the room that had become stiff with silence. I was hot and dizzy. My speech was confused, and my mind was going in all directions. This couldn't be happening! I began to think; you had just started college. We had just lost our house, and you didn't even have a room in that tiny little apartment—we had not even told you we moved! What about our plans to be in a new house in six months and to surprise you with a new room full of new furniture! What about my plans to go back to school! Josh would be starting middle school! What about football practice with Josh! And then there were projects at work! We just paid all that money for college tuition, books, and housing. As these thoughts without substance flooded my mind, without any forethought, I blurted out words to the entire family that came from somewhere other than my true consciousness. I selfishly announced in so many words that I wasn't going through this alone, that they needed to be here to help us. I went on to tell everyone how we'd lost our house and your dad had lost his job! Chris, I am sure you were already in shock, and then there I was losing my mind . . . At some point, I had drifted to Elgin and was in his arms; I felt him let me go and storm out of the room. He was infuriated. How could I say all those things and belittle him? Then I was in the hallway and must have lost consciousness. I came to the nurses break room. My parents were standing over me along with a doctor and a nurse all of whom were calling my name. They said I'd had some kind of "pseudo-seizure." Some mother. I should have been holding my child, trying to comfort him—what was wrong with me? I guess I too was in shock.

The days that followed were hard. They started chemotherapy almost immediately while you were in the hospital. You continued to experience bone pain and was taking a lot of pain medicine that made you sleep a lot, and when you were awake, you were not yourself. My heart was broken. I was shattered. Your dad and I were at odds. There was all this medicine to buy. I was being pulled in several directions all at once.

After you were released from the hospital, you had to stay with your grandmother so you could have a bed to rest in. Therefore, I was back and forth. You would eventually find yourself in and out of the hospital, just as the oncologist had explained. I would leave work to take you back and forth to your treatments. Fortunately, we had the help of your grandparents with getting Joshua to school and picking him up in the afternoons. Your dad had just started a new job so he couldn't take time off from work without losing pay.

When you began to lose your hair from the chemotherapy, your auntie Terri gave you the cutest gift. It was a mirror with a star on top with the words "You're a star." It had a matching coffee mug that read "Mr. Wonderful." Both really described you quite well. Despite the illness and all the thoughts that constantly went through your mind, you remained positive! How "wonderful" is that! Your entire demeanor in those early days inspired me to chronicle the events. So I began a journal entitled "Mr. Wonderful." In it, I kept up with your moods, medications, doctor's appointments, consultations, everything! I'd watch you sleep and write down your movements. I don't know why I kept up with every little aspect of things, I just did. I felt compelled to write it all down. I now know that this was merely a coping mechanism. It made me feel like I was doing something to help you. I wrote down everything. I made a schedule of your treatments and chronicled your medications along with the side effects. I knew I had to organize things to keep track of it all. I thought to myself, I can do this. I've faced challenges before. I just need to organize things, keep a clear head, and remain in control!

As a mom, we usually pick our children up when they fall. Almost instantly, a hug and a kiss soothes the pain away, and they are all better. But all the kisses and hugs in the world couldn't change where we were during those moments, hours, and days that followed.

Chapter 5

The Days Ahead

February 27, 2006

Dear Chris,

It's the end of February. Two months have gone by since the day our lives took this turn. I started a log to keep up with all this. It looks like the one I did for your dad back in 1997. It starts with day 1. I list your actions, your medications, your appointments. I'm not sure why I'm doing this—I guess, in part, it's to keep things organized, or maybe someday, when this is over, I can go back and figure out why it all happened in the first place. Maybe, in time, it will be revealed.

As for today, it's like most days, either you have a doctor's appointment or lab work. Many days, we find ourselves in the emergency room. It's funny, but during some of those visits, I almost wanted them to check me out too—it's this stupid tooth! I didn't tell you, but when you became ill, I was having some dental issues—I was supposed to have a root canal, and then this disgusting abscess developed. I know, nasty, right? I looked like there was a marble embedded in my face. I had been procrastinating because the dentist's office is absolutely one of my least favorite places to go. Anyway, they have me on this pain medicine. So between the medicine and the throbbing pain, I am a bit dazed and tired. We are at the hospital right now. You were brought in by ambulance last night. We had talked and said good night. Your grandmother later called to say you were having chest pains. It's been a blessing that you were able to stay at your grandparents' house, but I really wish we could all just be home together. I prayed all the way to the hospital. I was suddenly reminded that I have to pray without ceasing. You are growing agitated—telling me it's always something and that you always seem to have to work twice as hard to get half as much. I understand and I know this is frustrating. But God has a plan for your life. Maybe all of this is happening to help you appreciate life—laugh more, live and enjoy yourself more. You have always been so mature and serious-minded. You worry about me and your brother. Understandably so, things haven't been the easiest for our family. Your dad and I have been working hard to get things right so you can relax and be happy.

Dear Chris

You are a man now, and I pray for God's forgiveness that you lost so much of your childhood due to our issues. I try not to blame myself. Anger and frustration without an outlet can lead to illness; I wonder if this is some kind of manifestation. Even so, I continue to trust God. All things work together for His greater good.

They just finished more lab work and an EKG. Your heart rate has been elevated. You have been complaining about a sticking pain when you swallow and breathe in. Lord, I know all of this is making you weary. There is so much medicine to take, pain, side effects. It is a lot to deal with. You keep apologizing, but none of this is your fault, baby. I pray that we all have strength through this and not become selfish, considering the inconvenience of it all. You are the only one who deserves to be selfish right now—we are here for you.

Okay, it is now 5:00 a.m., and after much prayer over a possible blood clot, the ER doctor says it's acid reflux. Looks like we get to go home! More meds, but we'd get to go home! More often than not, the ER visits lead to hospital stays. We will have to see what your oncologist thinks we should do next. Rather than waking your grandparents, we decided to take you home with us. The apartment isn't very roomy, but it is home for now. It was your first time over, and you said it felt like home. Perhaps it was the familiarity of seeing all our things again, the pictures, etc. I guess it is true what they say, a home is not just a building. It is wherever you are with the people you love. It is also the place where you are most comfortable handling your business in the bathroom, and you did much better than you have in the past few days, my dear boy! I am glad your stomach is feeling better.

Chapter 6

Some Nurses Are Really Angels

March 1, 2006

Dear Chris,

T he home nurses are a blessing. But they each have varying opinions that baffle me. We are going to have to stay on top of things ourselves, sweetheart. One says to give you a certain medicine for nausea, the other disagrees. And then the hospital and clinic nurses have clashing opinions. It can be confusing, and I don't like this trial and error method of making you comfortable. I want to educate myself more on leukemia. Between all the running back and forth to the hospital, work, your grandparents' house, and all, I am about worn-out!

So many people are affected by this disease. The infusion center was filled with patients today. I went back to the car to wait for you and fell asleep; the nap actually made me more tired. I am trying to figure out how to plan our lives around this. I initially thought I could work half days during your infusion times, but then, there is traffic, the wait to be seen by the doctor, not to mention the occasional overnight sickness that keeps us up. Oh, and the frequent visits to the emergency room for stronger pain control. Your grandparents are helping out a lot, but I have to be at their house with you when the home nurses come. I have to leave home in the middle of the night to come take you for emergency room visits. I wish I could just bring you home, but I know you are more comfortable at your grandparents' house rather than the apartment.

Well, that is enough complaining for now. I have a praise report! Your dad is back at work! Yep, he started a new accounting job! Today was his second day. Lord knows we really could use another paycheck. Cancer is expensive; we are broke! I am not sure how we will manage over the next few days—just leaning on the Lord.

I am also praising God because you have had some good days, despite the pain and nausea. One day, we were watching music videos on television, and you were singing along with the music. You said you were considering a new outlook on life. I never thought I'd appreciate your sarcasm, but every now and again, it lets me know that you are handling this. You looked at me a few minutes ago and asked if I had much sleep last night because I seem "out of it." Wonder what gives you that impression?

They are selling doughnuts today for the March of Dimes. One of the volunteers is a member of our church. She gave us a warm hug as she received our donation and told us that they were praying for us. I received that. Despite the hurt, sadness, bouts of depression, concerns over our finances, etc., I feel somewhat encouraged. It really lifts me up when someone genuinely reaches out to us, just to say hello or give a hug; it can really make a difference. Something inside tells me everything is going to be okay. We just have to stay focused.

You had fever today of 102.5. Your infusion clinic nurse Janine took care getting a chest x-ray and lab work done. I don't know if this is routine due to fever, but her down-home nature and sincere gestures always make me feel as if she is going an extra mile or two for you. You and your usual charm really work a number on all your nurses. Even in this illness, you can be funny, witty, and charming. Janine is so patient with you. You just asked her for the third time what platelets are. She explains, again with a smile, as if it were the first time you asked, that blood platelets are formed by our bone marrow. They are the sticky substance along other parts of the blood that help to form clots to keep us from bleeding. Yours have been low so she has to give you more. Some of the nurses haven't been so pleasant, but for the most part, they are all angels.

Chapter 7

Blood Transfusion

March 3, 2006

Dear Chris,

I stayed home from work today; I was so tired. So I thought I would take some time to try to rest. I have been driving the "Green Bandit," the name affectionately coined by your dad for your cute little Mazda. By the way, it really needs to be serviced. Anyway, I slept off and on most of the morning. I couldn't focus on much when I woke up. I went from laundry to cleaning to sorting through bills. Needless to say, I didn't accomplish much.

Your dad wrapped up his first week at his new job. He was tired but insisted on picking your brother up from your grandparents and coming with me to see you at the hospital. When he got here, he started to feel ill, and we all had to leave early. He really doesn't like being at the hospital for long; I think it reminds him of his own battle with cancer—it's behind him now, and he doesn't want any reminders.

When we got to the hospital to see you today, my heart sank when I walked into the room. You were having your first blood transfusion, and I wasn't there to hold your hand when it started. I know you have been concerned about this, maybe a bit scared. So for me not to be there as you endured it for the first time was heart wrenching. This was a real transfusion. I had become familiar with the platelet bag, but to see the blood bag hanging there, it was surreal. Just when I think my mind is getting accustomed to all of this, I am reminded of the harsh seriousness of it all.

I unpacked some things for you, the usual underwear, etc. Your grandmother sent a recording of the Bible on tape that you have been listening to at her house. I had hoped to be able to spend time with you and help you bathe. But since your dad isn't feeling well, we have to leave. I don't like you being alone so much at the hospital. Your dad and I are both concerned about the transfusion. I wonder how or if it will affect you. I know your doctor is doing what he thinks is best to move swiftly toward recovery. And while I can't begin to fully understand the process of it all, I have to trust that God is directing everyone involved. I fully trust Him.

In my efforts to understand all this, I admit to being somewhat of a busybody. I know you must have overheard me trying to tell your nurses how to administer your meds, and you are agitated with me about it, especially when you called tonight after we got home to report that you had received a shot in your stomach. I insisted on talking to your nurse so she could explain this to me, but I relented after you said in the voice you use when you're agitated with me, "Ma, you gotta let these people do their jobs." I know you don't want me to undermine anybody's intelligence. That certainly is not my intention. I just love you so very much, and I need to know everything that's going on. Surely the doctors and nurses must understand that. They must deal with us busybodies regularly enough to have built up some sort of resistance or something!

Your dad and your brother prayed with me tonight. It was our first prayer together in a while. It felt good; I hope it happens more often. I asked that the Lord bless you tonight and give you sweet peace and rest. I prayed that the blood that flowed through the transfusion would help to strengthen your mind and your body, empowering you to continue to weather this storm. And I prayed the first of many prayers to come for the ones who so graciously respond to the call to donate blood and blood platelets.

Chapter 8

Hope Holds Faith

March 5, 2006

Dear Chris,

Looks like it's going to be another weekend at the hospital. You were scheduled for the bone marrow biopsy tomorrow, but it was delayed because apparently there is another infection. On Friday, when we got home from the infusion center, you were having upper abdominal pain. Then you became "teeth chattering" cold. You had a temperature of 101.5. Your doctor was paged, and at his discretion, he wanted you to stay and receive the nightly antibiotics you have been taking. You were readmitted to the hospital around eight fifteen this morning.

After we got you settled into your room, I went home and fell asleep. I woke up around two forty-five this afternoon. Your dad was very considerate of my need for rest. He picked your brother up from school, and they spent the rest of the day together. We all came back here to the hospital to visit you. Your brother was playful, but he is hurting inside. He and I went for a walk around the hospital, and he told me that he is very sad for you and afraid of something happening to you. Of course, I tried to reassure him. I also tried to explain that we don't know why things like this happen. We just have to trust God and hold on to our hope that things will get better.

The pastor preached a lively sermon about faith yesterday. He reminded us that faith is the substance of things hoped for, the evidence of things unseen; hope upholds faith. Josh heard him say that, and we looked at each other and smiled. There was a guest choir who sang "His Eye Is on the Sparrow." This was a gentle reminder of God's watchful eyes on you.

I came back to the hospital by myself this evening because you have been running a constant fever. It is at 103 right now. Earlier, they said your white blood count was up, but your hemoglobin is low, so you will be getting two more units of blood tonight. But they can't start until the fever goes down. You've also had a steady headache, believed to be attributed to your blood pressure being elevated. Earlier it was 156/94.

Dear Chris

It's getting late, sweetheart. I have to get home. It is so hard to tear myself away from you, baby. You are sleeping now; you have been dozing in and out since I got here. I wonder if you know I'm here or if you will wake up when I leave and think you were dreaming that I was here. I pray, the Lord bless you, my sweet baby, as you sleep tonight.

I sing because I'm happy—I sing because I'm free
His eyes are the sparrow—That's the reason why I sing
Glory Hallelujah
You're the reason why I sing

Chapter 9

It's Always Something

March 7, 2006

Dear Chris,

It's 9:15 a.m. You will be going down shortly to take an upper endoscopy exam. The doctor appears to be quite capable. You and I just prayed over this procedure and for the doctors and nurses involved. They explained the procedure involves looking down your throat with a camera. You have been complaining about abdominal pain.

Your doctor and I spoke briefly this morning. He says your counts are up, but he is concerned about monocytes in your white blood cells. They are really high, which causes further concern about the leukemia. He hopes to be able to do the bone marrow biopsy tomorrow. You still have fever. Your body is really fighting something. In the midst of your being groggy from the prep work for the endoscopy, you are pretty alert.

I dropped your dad and brother off before coming to the hospital this morning. Your dad and I—whew!—we can't seem to get on one accord. Sometimes he irritates me so much. Last night, he wanted me to ask the nurse "if we should expect something catastrophic to happen . . . so nobody is surprised if it does." Drama! You know the usual way he says stuff, but I won't even go into it today.

I know you are going to be agitated with me because you didn't want any visitors this time. Sweetie, just because you have been in and out of the hospital so often doesn't mean that people won't want to come see you. I know you are tired of being in here, and you don't want to inconvenience people. But so many folks care and want to show they are thinking about you. I asked your auntie Terri to come so she could be here when the procedure is over. I can only stay until they take you into the procedure room; I have to get back to work. Honestly, I am debating as to whether or not I should even go into the office. Then I wonder if I am making any difference by being here. I pray that you know I am here as much as I can be and that I am fully supporting you in all this.

41

Dear Chris

Kathy is your nurse today; she's a nice red-haired lady. She always seems flustered and in a hurry like she's running behind on something. I almost hate to ask her questions because I don't want to confuse her. It's eleven thirty-five, and we are in the recovery area. The doctor says the sedation they gave you would cause temporary amnesia, so you won't immediately remember the procedure. That may not be a bad thing; we could all benefit from some temporary loss of memory from this whole ordeal.

Funny, the other day, I almost wondered if every day I should ask, "What today, Lord?" Were you right when you said to me, "It's always something"? When you said that, it lingered in my mind. The procedure reveals there are five ulcers in your esophagus, and you have gastritis.

Chapter 10

Springtime and Family Moments

March 17, 2006

Dear Chris,

Yesterday, your dad and your brother and I decided to take some time out together. We went to a nature park in Palmetto, Georgia. We are thinking of buying a house there. It was nice having a break, but I couldn't really enjoy myself without you there too. A part of me is just empty when you are not around.

You looked good when I got to the hospital to visit you today. You said that you had been nauseated, tired, and having chest pain. Your appetite is good, but I am concerned about your not eating many vegetables. I am also wondering about bottled water. I have been doing my own research (Yes, I know your oncologist has asked me to stop trying to become a doctor and let him do his job).

But nonetheless, I think I should understand this. The problem is there is so much information out there. I wish there were one factual document that fully summarized everything. Something approved by the medical and spiritual community—one unified document and not these billions of opinions confusing people. I have read so much, and it's making me paranoid about everything. I can't continue to use the little energy I have on it—it's too much. I just want to give my energy and focus to you. Your oncologist is right; I can't expect to learn in a few hours on the Internet what he has studied for years. I suppose I am again forced to put some faith behind my prayers and trust God. I prayed for the best doctor for you, and people around here seem to think that you have the best.

Your doctor was in and out so quickly this morning. I totally forgot to ask all the questions I had written down! This was my new system to keep up with my concerns: write it down—Goodness, how could I have forgotten that? Late last night, you called to say you loved me. You were tearful and scared. I tried to encourage you; we praised God together, and I prayed myself to sleep while pretending that you were lying next to me in my arms. So of course, I looked forward to seeing you today. I was encouraged to hear that your blood counts are up! You had to receive more platelets, but the doctor says things are where they should be. He thinks the persistent nausea may be due to your pain meds and will try something new to see if you can get some relief.

After a bit of prodding—okay, threatening you—I finally convinced you to get out of bed. I had literally sat watching you sleep all morning. We went for a walk around the hospital around lunchtime. We stopped and looked out the window. It is springtime, my favorite season of the year. It signifies rebirth and regeneration. There were blossoms on the trees. It's funny I normally notice the season changing; I hadn't until that moment. You were in somewhat of a daze as you gazed out the window. Your eyes began to water, and I put my arms around you, gave you a squeeze, and whispered, "You will be out there again." And I know you will. You will be just fine. God will heal you.

After our walk, you took a shower and got back into bed. One of your best friends and self-adopted "little sister" came by for a visit. You really seemed to perk up while she was here. After she left, you said you really didn't want many visitors. I know it is hard for you to have your friends see you this way, but I truly believe that the positive energy of others helps. I know you communicate electronically with your friends every day, and most likely, you are telling them not to visit. I am glad this one ignored you and came anyway. True friends are easy to identify; they are the ones who stick around through thick and thin. They remind you of who you are inside and make you smile even when you don't want to. When they look at you, they see your heart.

I am proud of you. You finished your first round of chemo, a full regimen. It has been thirty-seven days since you were diagnosed and all the treatment started. Highlights of the past thirty-seven days have included the following: biopsies, pain medicine, transfusions, emergency room visits, and hospital stays. We have been dealing with the side effects: nausea, infections, etc. It's funny when we started the chemo sessions; we were happy your hair didn't come out. You always had thick curly soft jet-black hair. It's probably because of me that you paid so much attention to your hair. Over your whole life, we always talked about our hair. So when the doctor explained the hair loss as a side effect of the chemo, you and I both professed that it would not happen to you. We joked about it to cover up our fears over it actually happening. Then one day, it started coming out. Your dad and I noticed it while visiting you at the hospital. You had started sleeping on a towel because you were sweating a lot. The towel had pulled a lot out, and it was looking patchy. You and your dad both agreed to just cut it. Elgin brought his clippers and cut it down nicely for you. It was the one of the few touching moments I had seen between the two of you since this illness began. He took such care in every stroke as he gently cut and lined it up for you. We each had a touching hair moment with you. Prior to your haircut and before the patchy loss started happening, you and I were in the infusion center one day. You asked for my hand. I thought you were about to do something sweet, like hold my hand and tell me you love me. Instead, you scratched your head and handed me a patch of your hair. Before you had the opportunity to become somber about it, I plucked out a strand of my own hair and asked if you wanted to trade. In that smug sarcastic way of yours, you looked—gave me a funny look, and said, "Eh, no." We both laughed until we cried.

Chapter 11

I Love Our Texting Game

March 24, 2006

Dear Chris,

I didn't get to finish my last letter; I was too tired and had not enough time in the day. You were released from the hospital today. We are on our way home right now. You have truly been blessed! We all have. The results of the bone marrow were inconclusive. No evidence of leukemia cells! You doctor wants to err on the side of caution and do another bone marrow biopsy next week. He is being cautiously optimistic. I already started praising God. I truly believe you are healed. We are in the midst of the "text game"—where we silently communicate unbeknownst to your dad. I must admit, I do enjoy it a bit. It's like a secret world where only you and I exist. I know, weird, huh? We have been going back and forth for a while about a burger and fries. I really want you to eat healthier. But I do understand your craving after enduring several days of hospital food. Maybe you will eat in moderation, but you can be so stubborn, and your usual moodiness is currently at its peak, so I'm going to keep quiet; I don't want to upset you. I'm so glad we are going home today. There will be another round of chemo in about a week, so I want you to enjoy eating as much as possible. Since we have been on the highway headed home, your stomach has been rumbling. We had to pull over twice to let you hurl.

Your grandma Betty just called. Her pastor came to see you today. This is all so hard on her. You know she loves you so much and literally cannot stand to see you in any level of pain.

Chapter 12

You Are a Fighter!

March 29, 2006

Dear Chris,

We have been waiting all day for your oncologist to give us the news. What will the results of the bone marrow biopsy be this time? I think it's the fourth one since this whole ordeal started. This time, the procedure was done in the doctor's office, so I was allowed to stay in the room with you. I must admit part of me wished I had left the room. I thought I'd be able to write down a description of this event, but I'd rather not relive it. There was one point during the procedure where the doctor expected you to say ouch, but you barely flinched. He kind of chuckled as he commented to me that you never say anything. This didn't surprise me; I just thought to myself, *Yep that's typical of my baby.* You just lay there with your eyes closed. I figured you were in silent meditation, your mind far-off in another place. Then I recalled, when as a child you were admitted to the hospital for the first time. It would be the first of several asthma-related hospitalizations. You were only five years old. I sat there powerless as it took two nurses and a doctor to hold you down as they inserted an IV into your arm. I remember the flood of tears that filled your eyes. The guilt still riddles me as I reflect upon my inability to shield you from pain—déjà vu. There would be many more moments like that. As you got older, you became immune to needles. But with each instance, there was always a faraway look in your eyes.

Enough with gloomy thoughts! I'm happy right now because you have been feeling great for the past few days! There are some moments when you have expressed not feeling altogether and being a bit tired, but overall, you have been feeling good. It's so nice to hear you laugh again. You have been your usual witty self.

Tonight I cooked fried chicken, homemade fries, corn, and your favorite corn-bread muffins. You really enjoyed it. It felt really good to see you eating like your old self. I had hoped we could all eat together, but your brother had a difficult day at school and was moody. So we stayed in the kitchen together while you enjoyed your special dinner watching your favorite TV show, *Law & Order.*

Dear Chris

Your doctor finally called; baby, you're in your first remission! This is such good news because it means the chemo worked. However, it also means we have to continue with the treatment plan, which means five more rounds. When I initially heard the news of remission, I was so happy and grateful. I just praised God. You chose to be cautiously optimistic. You became somewhat agitated because I shared the news with your grandparents. But, sweetheart, they deserve to hear some good news. They all love you so much. I really wanted them to know that you are on the road to recovery. Your oncologist said if we didn't make the first remission, the odds of reaching the status of cure would be lessened.

I know that hearing five more rounds and "possibly" returning to school in the fall only further agitated you. But despite all that, we have been having some really good conversation; you keep me laughing. I know this has been hard for you, but you have always been a fighter. Your dad and I were happy you decided to hang out with us recently for dinner and a movie. It was a good distraction. On the way to the theater, I did my usual job as referee between you and your dad. It's amazing how the two of you can go at each other even in the midst of all this. We still managed to enjoy some time together.

In just a few days, we will celebrate your nineteenth birthday! You continue to be in good spirits, and your appetite has been normal—you're eating a lot, and that makes us all happy. You hardly look like you've been sick at all. You have decided that you only want to eat pizza and watch the Lakers game. It's also Easter time. In a perfect world, we would normally be planning for church, new suits for you and your brother, and a big family dinner complete with chocolate cake and nineteen candles. I am so proud of you. You have a positive outlook. You made up your mind to go back to school and not let this illness dictate your life. A few weeks after the final chemo, you returned to Georgia Southern. As you drove off, I felt a release in my spirit. I had planned not to cry, but the tears flowed anyway. The moment was surreal. This was your first real attempt to get past this illness and reclaim your life. Suddenly, there was no sadness, no regrets, and no worries.

Chapter 13

Keep Starting Again

August 12, 2006

Dear Chris,

I was on the phone with Georgia Southern again today. Despite all we went through to pay the balance on your account, they have taken you off the roll. I was able to speak with a very helpful person in the student fees office. She agreed to help with a reinstatement. I know you are frustrated—I got all your text messages about dropping out. I have been trying to be encouraging to you, but I too am starting to wonder if it's really worth all this hassle!

I know you have been having more pain in your legs. You were so determined to get back to school. Now with all these issues with financial aid, I wonder if the additional stress may have triggered something. In addition to that, I know you are also worried about your dad, as well as me and Josh. I really don't want you to have to come back home. But if you do, you can try again.

I recently received my first copy of this magazine by Joyce Meyer *Enjoying Everyday Living*. My assistant at work recommended it to me. As I flipped through the pages, there it was again. That scripture, Jeremiah 29:11. You may recall someone handed it to me when we started dealing with this mess. Until I read it today, I figured it meant just what it says, "God knows His plans for me." But Joyce's interpretation said, "He has a great future planned for you." I am holding on to this message. As I drove to the hospital with your dad today, I pondered over my usual list of issues and thought to myself, surely my life was not meant to be just this: back and forth to hospitals, illness, uncertainty about finances, and the inability to remotely plan for my future. Now I am beginning to see that God's plan is obviously bigger and more powerful than anything I could come up with. So I will do my best to live one day at a time and enjoy it!

Your dad and I just got back from his ultrasound appointment. The technician tried to act as if she was just doing her job, but I couldn't help but notice an air of concern. It was obvious she didn't want us to see the report. She kept it facedown while we waited. You know I have been through this procedure several times, and that's not normal. Well, no matter what, I know that God is in control.

I must confess that I didn't want to come back to the hospital today. I am thinking about the wear and tear on my car. I just wanted to go to work today. Elgin had me up all night. He was talking in his sleep again and occasionally waking up in agonizing pain. When God brought us through this sickness ten years ago, I knew I never wanted to endure this again. It is hard taking care of him. He is such an intense person. Under normal circumstances, with the routine issues of life, he is difficult. He often misinterprets things I say. We are often in disagreement and at odds with each other. So you can imagine under these circumstances, his negative disposition is magnified. I don't mean to complain so much. Selfishly, I admit, I know I have had to deal with a lot, and I am not asking for any worldly accolades, just a little respect—heck, just a bit of admiration from my husband would be nice.

Praise God! The ultrasound looks good according to the doctor. Apparently, there is some fluid around the lining of the testicle, but supposedly, this is normal. The doctor suspects that the tumor is pinching a nerve that is radiating pain in the scrotum area. (I know, "TMI," too much information, but this is my letter, right?) Thankfully, your dad doesn't have to be readmitted this time. I am glad the Ole Grouch is coming home.

Sweetie, just as you are trying again, so am I. I went back to work again today. My heart wasn't there. It hasn't been for quite some time. I am truly thankful for my job and especially my coworkers. I do enjoy my work. I'd just like to get back to happiness. I miss the days of carpooling with your dad, discussing our day, occasionally having lunch together. I would look forward to coming home to you and your brother playing outside in the yard. Our lives have taken on a whole new reality. And back to that reality, your dad did well tonight. He was in bed when I got home from work. He had taken all his medicines and eaten bread all day. He told me he got his car detailed today. I knew that against all orders, he would drive somewhere. Thank goodness he didn't get into an accident! I was a bit nervous about leaving him at home alone.

Well, one last note about trying again. You would be so proud of your brother. He is growing into quite a fine young man. When I woke up this morning, he had cleaned his room and organized his clothes for the week. He is trying to do what he can to help out. Hopefully, he and I will be seeing a play this weekend. We are also starting research for his science project. We just wrapped up a social studies project on Canada. You know I had my usual suggestions for a guaranteed A project. He scoffed at my idea to offer samples of Canadian bottled water for extra points. Both of you always say I go overboard with your projects, and maybe I do—you have to stand out from the competition. But no thanks needed for all those As, baby boy. Seriously though, I am holding your brother extra close. I don't want him to get lost in the midst of these trials.

Chapter 14

Why Ask Why?

September 9, 2006

Dear Chris,

I t's barely been two weeks since you returned to school, and you have begun to call home from school complaining about pain again. To top it off, we just found out that your dad's cancer has also returned. He had been complaining a lot about being more tired than usual and of his back pain. He was suddenly losing weight. We joked about it all being due to his new sports car. That cute little red Corvette is hot (literally) with all that black leather. We are both sweating profusely when we get out of it. We found ourselves back at the infusion center this morning. The front desk staff looked at me with great concern as I walked in. They all asked, "Where is Chris?" Sadly, I replied that I was there with another patient—my husband. For a tenth of a second, I felt their pity; I immediately ignored it. I made up my mind right then and there that it would not be a pity ride for me. I'm not even asking why. Why ask why? Where does it get you other than hurt and confused? No, I am bigger than this. I will keep my head up. I have to stay up.

When we entered the infusion center, your sweet nurse Janine was there, humming those loving Negro spirituals. You know you keep me laughing even when you're not around. Okay, admittedly, neither of us actually knows what those tunes are, but somehow when she hums, it brings about calmness. I guess that's why you one day started calling it "old Negro spirituals"—too funny. Elgin is actually assigned to another nurse, but it was nice of Janine to get us started. She didn't ask us any questions or look at me with pity. She just picked up your dad's chart and started the meds. I really appreciated that because the same tears that I held back at that moment, I can now let flow as I write. As she prepared the medicines, she explained the process. She started with the first medicine, Taxol. Your father joked, "I hope it doesn't tax all." You know those morning allergies he has that cause his eyes to water? Well, they were watering when he said that. Of course, Janine thought he was literally crying. (I kind of chuckled to myself because I'm always messing with him about

51

that.) Anyway, Janine, being considerate of what she thought were tears, decided to lighten things up a bit by talking about you. She wishes you the best at school. After a brief breather, she reopened the chart, noting the thickness of your dad's patient records. Your father noticed that he was sitting in the same seat as he had in 1997. Honestly, this entire experience is unbelievable.

Last night, your dad had to do his premeds. They were scheduled for 9:00 a.m. and 3:00 a.m. So needless to say, I didn't get much sleep. I am grateful to be here for you and your dad. I shudder to imagine what it must be like for anyone to be alone and have to endure all this while also keeping up with the scheduling of everything. Anyhow, I had little to no sleep last night. I had this weird dream when I finally did doze off. In the dream, I was on a train, and then I was in this beautifully landscaped backyard. My mom appeared and told me that she asked someone to marry me so that I wouldn't be alone. The guy was a nerd, and the marriage didn't work out. Then there was another scene in the dream where your other grandmother was sitting alone. Your brother turned to you, and I heard a voice saying, "Someone needs to take care of Grandma." After that, I found myself in a pet store, and there was a cat that kept getting out of its cage and trying to come to me. The pet-store worker kept putting him back in the cage, but it continued to meow as if it were trying to talk to me. You know I have the craziest dreams when I am deprived of sleep! And you are often my trusty ear when I need to share; although I know you are truly ignoring most of my dream madness, I do appreciate you acting as if you are listening.

The infusion center can get really cold. I had to step out for a minute. The other night, I allowed myself to have a really good cry. Since all this happened, my heart has been so heavy with sadness. I am trying to find my joy, but it's hard. There was a lot of traffic on the way to the center. As we inched along, I thought about how we can approach a situation with dread, and then it becomes dreadful. What if we approached situations with joy? Could they become joyful? I pray to God, and in every attempt, I try not to ask why? All my hopes and desires are on hold because of all this. But I know there must be a reason for it all. I may not ever know the reason why. I can only hope and pray for the greater good to come of it all.

When your dad became ill, I began to truly realize how much I love and need him. I wish I could take back all the petty arguments, misunderstandings, and anger. I wish I could go back and just love him, accept him, and just enjoy being near him. I imagine us being older, settled—having everything together. As I close my eyes, I can see us settled, traveling, enjoying the holidays. I see us smiling as your brother leaves for his first date. Holding hands as we host your engagement dinner party—um, yes, I am planning for that. And then there's our grandchildren, little Christina and—well, I haven't named Josh's son yet. But I am pretty certain that you will give me a granddaughter. You know, I have these thoughts often. They help me to stay focused on tomorrow.

I know it's not going to be easy from this point on. I never could have imagined both you and your dad being sick at the same time. Your dad isn't the easiest to handle when he's not feeling well. When he was ill ten years ago, I thought I was going to lose my mind! He can be so demanding, overbearing, and downright rude. Even though I am constantly by his side, if he falls asleep and wakes up to find me gone, he immediately acts as if I have abandoned him. But I love my husband. So I am not going to let him get to me this time. I am a pillar of strength because I am doing all this through Christ! Let's hope Christ doesn't need any help—you know I don't drink, but I can already see myself possibly needing something other than the Holy Ghost—spirit! I just have to keep reminding myself that God has a plan. He must! I pray things will indeed change for the better. I pray that when we get through all this, our family is much stronger and closer.

As I write, I am concerned about you. You have been thinking about quitting school since the pain started coming back in your legs.

Chapter 15

The Load Gets Heavier

September 18, 2006

Dear Chris,

You are back home from Georgia Southern and back in the hospital. This time your dad is a patient too. He is completing his third round of chemo at Northside. Our prayer is that the fourth round will complete the necessary chemo although his doctor has planned for a total of six rounds. Elgin has lost a total of sixty pounds since he got sick. He is always nauseated and is unable to keep anything down, even water. He is now being fed through an IV. I have been trying to keep him comfortable, bathing him myself, even taking pleasure in washing his feet (I know, I know, TMI, too much information). Your dad can be easy to love sometimes, like when he is not in pain and heavily medicated! (LOL)

This week we learned that you will have to undergo a slow-release chemo in your spine along with radiation therapy on your neck. The leukemia cells returned in your spinal fluid, and so for the past few weeks, you have had blurred vision in your right eye and pain in your neck and right arm. The pain seems to intensify more and more each day. Yesterday it was so bad that you were sedated and placed in the ICU. The doctors explained that you have nerve pain, which is harder to control. The most they can do is try to keep you comfortable. It was hard seeing you in so much pain yesterday. You said you felt like you were on fire; you were screaming! The doctors suspect that the pain was a reaction from the chemo injection. The radiation is a five-day treatment. Today was day 2. I watched as the technicians placed you on a table and covered your face with a plastic netlike mask. There were laser beams to ensure you were properly aligned on the table underneath a large rotating machine. It was like watching a science fiction movie. I watched with unblinking eyes as the tech pushed a button. It all lasted for five minutes. I don't understand all that is involved in radiation therapy, but it was fast, and you acted as if you didn't feel a thing.

2007

And when the song is over—We've all said Amen
In your heart just keep on singing
And the song will never end!

Chapter 16

Where Is My Joy?

February 2, 2007

Dear Chris,

We are starting a new year. God has brought us so far. Despite the blessings, my life seems to spiral into confusion, financial problems, lack of focus, and I can't seem to stay happy.

I am very thankful for healing and grace. You and your dad have been doing very well. You both have staph infections, your dad more so than you. He has also developed a painful swelling in his left cheek. We were at the emergency room twice this week.

Your transfer to Morehouse College went well. It is good to see you happy again. The change has been somewhat challenging because of the fees. But you are so focused and determined to manage your way through the process. Tonight, during our usual good-night text messaging, you wrote to say you were in your dorm room completing an assignment. You really love your independence. I am so proud of you. I pray for God's continued blessings over you.

Your dad recently returned to work! He completed two full weeks, but then the infection started again. So he's been off for the past four days. It's been difficult without his income, but we've managed to stay afloat. We are quite blessed. Your brother is doing well at school. He was recently elected sixth grade vice president! His name was in the school newsletter today among the other student government officers. He did have a couple of rough days this week because of some "haters," but he got past it.

And praise God for our new home!!! Yes, we moved in just before Thanksgiving. Our house is so beautiful. What a blessing: five bedrooms, four full baths, two fireplaces, hardwood floors, marble—and ceramic-tile floors, and a great neighborhood! I could go on and on! God is so awesome—that's why I know—for Him to bless us with it. He will make a way for us to keep it. It's just that I was counting on your dad returning and staying at work. Sporadic paychecks—not good. Each night, I stay up praying and trying to come up with a plan. Everything costs; you have to spend money to make money. So tonight, I am again reminded that if I want something different to happen, I have to do something different. But what? I try not to succumb to fear. Your dad may have to have surgery, which means he will be off from work again. I want to try to earn more money, but with all these medical issues, it's best I stay put. It is so frustrating, like living in a maze and constantly running into brick walls—which way is out?

Our family is truly in some kind of battle. You have been having chronic pain in your shoulder. I noticed you have been holding your arm—kind of funny—when you walk. I am sure it's been going on for a while, but you've been bearing it because you want to move on and not have to stop school again. Looks like your recent MRI shows that the leukemia is back. A large mass has developed between your neck and shoulder. Since there is no match for a bone marrow transplant, your doctor thinks more chemo would do more harm than good. He is recommending radiation again and pain meds. He says there's not much else he can do. The last time he said that we all took it in stride. After all, you were pain free, no trace or indication of the illness. But it came back anyway. According to the doctor, it will continue to do so and show up or travel near your nerves. Sweetheart, your father and I are not giving up hope. We are trying to get you seen at MD Anderson in Houston. They are highly recommended. I wish we had started there, but this insurance business is a hot mess! If they put lives above dollars, I am sure there would be a larger cure rate among all cancers. MD Anderson is supposed to be the second-best cancer treatment center in the United States. I feel good about them; I did a lot of research. I don't want to waste any more time checking places. Then maybe again, I should do more research. I honestly don't know what to do. I have talked to so many people all with differing opinions.

Then there's your dad. Elgin is preparing for surgery to be done in Indiana. When we found out we would have to fly back and forth in preparation for this event, I didn't know how we would manage to afford it! We serve an awesome God. Thanks to the volunteer organization Angel Flight, we took our first flight together. I'd always hoped we would be able to travel together by flight. We had each only flown individually and only on business. So during the trip, I tried to encourage myself and your dad by acting as if we were on a much-deserved vacation. Last night, Josh had a paper to write. It was about defining moments based on a novel his class read. He wrote about how cancer affected him and his family. He cried as he read it to me and your dad. We cried inside as we listened. We have both been so so tired lately that tears barely flow on the outside anymore.

I am just trying to manage it all and hold on to our blessings. This sickness threatens us all. I will not stop trusting God; it's all I can do—it's all I truly have.

Chapter 17

Family Matters and Well-Wishers

March 23, 2007

Dear Chris,

Sometimes family can be the ones who are there for you the most and other times, the least. They know you from way back and forever see you for your past. For some, it's hard to look past what was then to now. So it's difficult for them to truly know how to help you when either they rarely helped before or they never had the opportunity to get to know where you currently are in your life.

Oftentimes as we grow older, we no longer cling to the mistakes of our past or need the advice of yesterday. Life either builds us up or tears us down. And if you live long enough, you will decide when you need people or when you don't. Imagine someone of great pride and independence who became an adult quite early in life and had to make their own way. That's who we were. So when you became ill, it wasn't easy listening to the advice of too many people. Elgin and I could both be quite stubborn. When we set our minds in one direction, it was like pulling teeth to get us off into another direction. With all we had been through, we could recognize sincerity. If someone came at us with polite gestures, we'd just accept them just as that. For years, we merely "circled the wagons" when we had family problems, as your father thought was best. We rarely allowed anyone else in because at the end of the day, we figured that all we really could rely on was each other.

As life's journey takes us down this road called cancer, we are learning to loosen the reins of our wagon's circle and open up more. We are forced to rely on the help of others. We have gotten a little comfortable in doing so, but at times, experience some levels of disappointment at some responses we received when we open up too much. Make no mistake; we love our family, and they have been a blessing. It's just that there are limits, and we respect that. But it's when you go through something that you often find out who is truly there for you and who is not. Cancer is hard. It's not just about the chemotherapy, radiation, and other drug treatments. I advise anyone who is going through this or someone who has a loved one going through it to pray for them and show (not just tell) them that you are there for them. A good friend of mine calls me every once in a while just to say hello. She always leaves a message when I don't answer the phone and says she is thinking about us. She goes on to say, when I feel like it, to give her a call. Recently, she offered to organize a help-out crew to come over to do laundry, cook dinner for us, and take Joshua to football practice. I pathetically declined with my foolish pride, but had she persisted, I probably would have been convinced to accept this generous offer. This friend understands that I need a break. She further understands that she need not be too persistent because she knows I will call if I need her. I feel her sincerity, and I do call her every so often, and we talk. She lets me babble on and on often about nothing in particular. These mental breaks are like thirst quenchers in the midst of a wide and lonely desert.

Then there is my mother-in-law, your grandmother—my goodness! How many married women can truly say they absolutely *love* their mother-in-law? I would venture to say, there is a nominal amount, and yet I am one of those fortunate few. My mother-in-law is some kind of an angel. Her home has always been a place of refuge for anyone in need. Back in 1997, she and your grandfather Hardy took us all in when your dad initially became ill. Now here we are with all of this, and she is right here for us as always, offering just the right amount of love that we need from her. She took care of you during some of your darkest moments. She made sure you had your meals (as you could tolerate them) and your medicines as they were scheduled. When she isn't nursing you guys, she is tending to her other grandchildren, Joshua and your cousin, Kayla. When she's all done with everyone else, she still finds time to provide encouragement to me.

When your dad found himself battling through cancer for the second time, her arms and home were wide open. She nurses him during the day so I can work, prepares meals so I don't have to cook, and continues to pick up our little Joshua from school. Although we also have assistance from our other family members, our mother, grandmother, friend, and confidant holds a special place in our hearts.

When you became ill and your dad and I found ourselves at odds with each other, it was her that brought us back to our senses and reminded us that our love for each other had to be stronger for us to get through all of what was in store for us. Over the years, she has taught us so much about what family means. Having been married for nearly fifty years, she is a model of a strong God-centered woman.

Chapter 18

I'm Okay until Someone Asks Me

March 28, 2007

Dear Chris,

All too often, I just want to be left alone. I don't want to deal with anyone because if I do, I simply fall apart and find myself in uncontrollable tears. I am beginning to feel as if cancer has taken over my life. I'm afraid to smile too much or allow myself to be too happy because whenever I do show the slightest bit of joy, there is cancer again with all its effects and sending us back to the emergency room.

I have experienced some selfish moments when my mind wonders why people seem to only call or write just to check on you and your dad. What about me? Doesn't anyone care that I am carrying this all alone? Don't they know I have put hundreds of miles on my car going back and forth to that hospital? Can they even imagine that I may have just spent good money on more pain medicine that my husband refuses to even take? Don't they know I must be tired—after all, I have been spending nights at a hospital designed only for some level of patient (not visitor) comfort? Don't they know that creditors couldn't care less if you are the only person working in your home; they still want their money? Will they just consider for a moment that maybe Val needs a break? Often this war inside my head keeps me from even answering the phone and responding to e-mails or any correspondence from family and friends. When people try to offer me words of inspiration or encouragement, I just see it as a waste of my time. After all, why would anyone think I even feel like reading some poem or scripture they've found—I'm too angry and tired to take time for what seems to be some insincere, pointless message? After all, they just can't possibly understand what I am going through. Do they really care, or are they just being polite out of some sense of obligation? I know they truly mean well and want to help. These selfish moments of mine come and go.

I know, family and friends are important. We should keep them close in our hearts. They are not perfect. They are not mind readers. They are merely human. Life is too short to allow indifference, shortcomings, and misunderstandings to

61

hinder your relationships. I pray that we all take the time to truly love and nourish our relationships. It's true that people come into our lives for a reason and a season. It's not just about you—God can lead someone to you for their benefit. So the most you can do is be the best person you can be. Your family and friends will certainly appreciate that.

Chapter 19

Almost Memorial Day

May 25, 2007

Dear Chris,

As the plane entered the sky, I could see Indiana below. I had to leave your dad there alone recouping from surgery. And here I am, high above, in flight between you and him. As we have struggled with these illnesses, I have often been conflicted with my time. Many times, I wished for a clone so I could be with you both at all times. I had told myself that if I ever had to be in one place, it would be an easy decision—I would be with you. It wasn't easy leaving your dad behind this time. But when I got the call to hurry home to you, I had no other choice. I can only trust that God is with us in the midst of all of this.

When I got back to Atlanta, I immediately came to the hospital to be with you. The doctors explained that they weren't sure whether you will make it much longer without a new procedure for chemo, which meant performing another risky surgical procedure.

I just kissed your cheek as they wheeled you into surgery. The doctors have come again to be certain that you have decided to move forward with the procedure. The procedure involves inserting a chemo reservoir into your head. What awaits us now as we go down this new chemotherapy road to treat your brain and central nervous system? My god! So much is happening all at once. I wish your dad were here, all healed and standing with me to hold your hand. But he will be home soon. I am torn because I don't want to leave you, but he will need me too when he returns to Atlanta.

I am praying for you, my love. I am asking God to lead you according to His plan. I know that the decision to continue to fight was a hard one for you because it means losing so much more time from school again and life in general. I know God is with us. He shows me more often than not. As I sit here alone trying to hold it together, the hospital chaplain just stopped by. He is much like the chaplain at the Indiana hospital, very soft-spoken, with a strong sense of calmness about him.

Chris, I try so hard to be this rock. People are calling, family, friends, etc. I do appreciate their prayers and concerns. My mind is often so divided. There are times when I am unable to speak. Too often, it's as if I have no communication skills at all. I open my mouth to speak, and it's not in sync with my brain. I stumble over myself and am often at a loss for words. So many of the calls from well-wishers simply go unanswered.

Praise God, the reservoir procedure went well! The scar looks exactly as the doctors described it. You came through the procedure with no difficulties; my goodness, you are amazing! You've been resting well and talking in your sleep. As I watch you in such peace, I am thankful for your rest. It's the only time you don't appear to be in pain. You woke up at one point with intense pain; I quickly called the nurses, and she explained it was normal after the procedure. I know you have also been upset about how some of the nurses are handling your pain control. It is just a shame that they are not all equally trained in how to deal with all that you're are facing. But I really do appreciate all the nurses. I can't imagine what they must go through on a daily basis with all the different needs of different patients.

You started the chemo again today. My heart ached for you when they started the new procedure. I knew your tears were filled with more anguish than pain. I could hardly find the words for one of my typical pep talks.

Your dad should be home by Memorial Day. That's right; it actually hit me today that this is a holiday weekend approaching. I suppose normally I would be making plans. You know my usual plans that never actually happen but are fun to think about, like putting steaks on the grill, shopping, weeding my flower beds, and getting some leisure reading time in. But what actually happens under normal circumstances is that I go back and forth with your dad about going on a nature hike, which is what he usually wants to do instead. As I ponder over these annual rituals, I am reminded of how we usually just find ourselves at the mall or at your grandma's house for dinner. This year, I am also finding myself in deep thought over the meaning of this holiday.

I am working my extra job this holiday weekend. I'll be at the Jazz and Caribbean Festivals. By the time my shift ends on Sunday night, Memorial Day will be a day of rest at the hospital with you and your dad, unless you both come home. There is a part of me that wants you both to come home, but I selfishly prefer that you stay where you can be well taken care of. You both have pain control issues that require IV medicines that are only administered in the hospital.

You have been in so much pain for the past few days, and you've hardly eaten much. Your hair came out again. I am praying that the Lord will give you some meaning to all of this. You have said to me that you feel as if you are not living, merely existing. You began counting the days of this hospitalization; this time it's been almost a month since you were admitted.

Yesterday, Josh and I washed my car and yours in the driveway. Our neighbors must really be wondering what's up with us. They've probably observed me and your brother out doing yard work with your grandfather; now here we are washing cars—you know, stuff your dad normally would be doing. One thing's for sure, I am definitely not one of those women who "doesn't need a man." I love all my men; I want to focus on my hair and nails again—you boys can have the pleasures of yard work and car washing!

Too often, I feel as if I too am merely existing and not living. I am going through motions like a machine to get through the day. I no longer know what it feels like to truly smile, to take a deep breath and feel the sensation of fresh air. Over the past few days, this roller-coaster ride has been twisting and turning in all directions: from our medical coverage being cancelled and reinstated, loss of wages, immunizations for Josh, and bills piling up. When will it all end?

So the days turn into nights, and I find myself alone in my bed. I never thought that I would know loneliness. For so long, I have been so strong; now I am finding myself in moments of weakness. I am beginning to wonder if there is indeed some correlation between one's thoughts and reality. I recently began to ponder the notion of each of you not coming home. What would I do if I found myself alone? You know me, always prepared. But how could I prepare for such a thing? I am almost fearful to write these words because I don't want to give life to loss. But I can only hope that in all my writing, I can sort things out somehow.

As I sit here alone with my thoughts, wondering about life, all I see are all the bills we have, the house payments that are behind, and the fact that you will not be enrolling in classes next term. I can only believe that nothing is too difficult for our Lord. I sarcastically ask the Lord again to forgive my selfishness in wanting you and your father to be healed and for not wanting us to lose everything we have because of these illnesses. I pray for further forgiveness for my sarcasm and am reminded that the redeemed of the Lord should say so and that God has given us His word regarding life and healing. When all is said and done, it will be by His will. So I pray for His mercy as I drift off to sleep.

Chapter 20

The Godfather

June 1, 2007

Dear Chris,

We have not been in this battle alone. We have friends and family who have blessed us with their time and their presence. You are indeed blessed with so many people who love you. Of course, no one can possibly love you more than me and your dad. There is someone who comes in at a close second, your godfather, Sam. I truly believe he is an angel on this earth. I don't know how I could have gotten this far without him. Since this whole ordeal, he has been right here. He stays with you at the hospital and takes care of you when I am unable. It doesn't matter what time of the day or night we call, he is there. The blessing in him is that he has always been here for us through the good and the bad. It is not often that one finds such a friend.

When I travel to Indiana with your dad for his treatment, Sam stays with you at the hospital. He was with you when the doctors escalated your condition to critical. Everyone was panicking about your breathing and running a temperature. Sam, being in his true form, was perfectly calm. He jokes about how you were rolling your eyes at the whole matter to put me at ease so I could calm down long enough to make emergency flight reservations to get back home from Indiana.

My favorite thing about Sam is his sense of humor. When I am ready to fall apart with my emotions, he seems to make me laugh and brings me back to my senses. He is so laid-back. He puts up with you and me and never expects anything in return. He is amazing: working, taking care of his own family, going to school, and making time to look after you. He has taught you so much. While he initially came into our lives as a mentor to you, he has done nothing short of being a mentor and role model for all of us. I pray that he and his family will always be a part of ours.

Chapter 21

Father's Day

June 15, 2007

Dear Chris,

It is 7:00 p.m. on a Thursday evening. They just wheeled you in for an MRI. You've had this procedure before, but this time, they need to be sure it would be done since you had the reservoir installed. They asked for the patient information card, and it occurred to me that when the procedure was done, I was so emotionally wrecked that I didn't get any information! This is so unlike me. Typically, I want to read everything, see pictures, etc. It also occurred to me that I had not finished writing this letter to you. I had stopped writing the day of the procedure. So here I sit in the radiology waiting room two months later. Wow, a lot has happened since then. You were actually discharged last Friday! Six weeks in the hospital this time. The leukemia came back stronger, but you proved to be even stronger. The doctors have been skeptical and cautious since you arrived on April 23. They advised us how risky the reservoir procedure would be; they were concerned about bleeding during the process. Then they were concerned about you making it through the induction therapy. Oh, and yes, they were also concerned that the chemo might not work. And of course, there's always the concern about infections. If you were to get one, it might . . . well, praise God. Well, you got through the induction therapy. You did get an infection, something called C diff. It was a nasty infection that altered your digestive functions, but you beat it. You are so remarkable; you managed to keep your appetite through the whole ordeal!

Sweetheart, it has been a long hard road. I have cried myself to sleep, anguished over all that you have had to endure. But we serve an awesome God! I know you are sad, frustrated, and you often feel alone. You have had to defer your dreams and question hope and faith. My dear son, you are stronger than you know. I have always sought for and drew from your strength. When I look into your eyes, I know it's all going to be all right.

Dear Chris

Father's Day will be here soon. I actually hoped that we could celebrate with a family barbecue at our new house. I had figured that by now your dad would have had his surgery, recuperated, and be just getting back on his feet. We would center the party around his healing. Well, things haven't quite turned out the way I had hoped. When your dad had his surgery, it was quite a bit more intense than we thought. They removed the tumor and everything attached to it, including his spleen, right kidney, part of his pancreas, and part of his lower intestine! Wow! Your dad is also something amazing. He too has been through a lot. His return home from Indiana was a traumatic experience for him. There was a crazy ride with a rude cabdriver who drove him to the airport. He was nauseated and in pain, which intensified while he was on the plane. It had been nearly two weeks since I had to leave him in Indiana so I could come home to be with you. During that time, he wasn't eating and lost a great deal of weight. He was home two days before we found ourselves back at the hospital, where he would be admitted for another month, with the exception of the one day when he convinced his sister to bring him home without medical approval. Your brother and I had just finished dinner when I heard the doorbell. I was angry and shocked to see his frail body walking into the house. He actually just wanted to shower and shave in his own bathroom, all the while extremely nauseated. I took him back to the hospital the next day. A few days after that, the cancer started spreading again. It was a devastating blow after the major surgery he endured. He was immediately started on chemotherapy again. After two days, he developed a dangerous bacterial infection called sepsis. But you know, we serve an awesome God! Your dad had to be admitted to the ICU; you see sepsis attacks the organs, starting with the kidneys. And since your dad only has one kidney, they needed to watch him closely. It was a Sunday morning when the doctor called me. I woke up that Sunday morning with the intent of making it a different day for us. We weren't going to be late for church. Your brother would not be made to suffer all the service in clothes that are too small. He can't control his preteen growth spurts, you know. I had purchased a new suit for him. I woke up early and even made breakfast! I know, pretty out of character, right? I actually had time to take a few minutes for myself to have breakfast on the deck. But my conscious incited me to check my voice mail. It was the doctor. He left his cell phone number! They never do that! It must be serious. Before returning the call, I took a deep breath and reminded myself that the enemy is not in control; God is. My God is in charge, and we honor Him by living by His word. So in my usual dignified way, I held my head up, and your brother and I continued to get dressed for church. I was scheduled to work my extra job that afternoon, but getting past my fear disguised as defiant dignity; I cancelled so I could be with your dad.

After church, I dropped your brother off at your grandparent's house and went to see your dad at the hospital. When I got there, he was shivering and not altogether coherent. They had provided a sitter for him overnight because he had been confused and was refusing treatment. I was so grateful for the sitter. It was difficult to see my husband—a man who had been so strong and virile—now at this stage. I read some scriptures to him and just talked to him. I just wanted him to hear my voice and come back to me. For a while, I sat quietly and just watched him, and after about an hour, he called out for me. My heart felt its familiar ache, and I had to step outside as my mind began to actually conceive the possibilities.

The doctor had come in and explained the situation again; they were watching him closely for kidney failure. I politely thanked the nurse and the sitter for their support and care. It seems the entire hospital staff knows me or knows about us. When they see me coming, I can read their thoughts—"there is the lady who has half of her family in the hospital; she practically lives here." Many of them just look as if they feel sorry for me; some are nice enough to take a moment just to say hi or offer a hug.

As I left the hospital today, I began to miss your father so much that my insides churned as my heart just began to sink. I continue to realize just how much I need him in our lives. I have been trying to rush his recovery, but today confirmed that this is a process that he has to go through. I then thought of you again, and the fact that you too are going through a process. I can't kiss you and make it all better. I am not in control. I thought I was, but I am not.

So happy Father's Day to your dad and my wonderful husband. You have a pretty terrific dad. Okay, so he can be a bit over the top at times, but I know he loves us very much.

And if somebody ask you was it just a show
Lift your hands and a be a witness
And tell the whole the whole world no!

Chapter 22

Healing for Dad?

June 28, 2007

Dear Chris,

I spoke to your doctor today. He is now the primary for your dad. He took over your dad's case because the other doctor has said there is nothing more that can be done and is recommending hospice care. Your doctor agreed to take over your dad's case, and he thinks he may be able to offer another chemo regimen; however, he isn't giving us any guarantees. When he called to explain the plan of treatment, he also provided an update on the alpha-fetoprotein level, which is the test to monitor tumor markers. In a very nonchalant way, he said the test was normal, which he suspected was an error and would need to be rerun. Inside myself I just began to praise God—could we have a miracle? I didn't ask any questions or comment. I just let the doctor go on with his report.

I quickly finished my lunch and went on through my hectic day at work, which flowed into the night as I had a community meeting. When I got home, I went through my usual lonely ritual of eating a crappy snack while sorting through mail and checking messages. I turned on TBN, and this young brother who has a church in Seattle was talking about resurgence. On my way home tonight, it was raining a much-needed rain in the midst of this current drought we've been experiencing. I thought about how you had told me that it was raining when they put you into the ambulance when you were transported home after the initial diagnosis. You went on to tell me that rain represented change. Of course, it has rained numerous times prior to tonight, but for some reason, the rain captured my attention. So anyway, the young pastor on TBN talked about the meaning of resurgence; he defined it as something that has already begun. "God is moving with resurgence in the people," he said. He went on to give an example of healing that had stopped and is being resurged—started again. And then I wondered, was this confirmation? I began to believe right then and there for your father's healing. God has brought your dad so far to this point of his faith and belief. He has been reaching out to God in an attempt to strengthen his relationship and seek God's direction for his life. I believe that God is honoring that. So I just pray that we can get on with whatever God has called us to do.

Chapter 23

Stuff People Don't See

July 1, 2007

Dear Chris,

It has been an exhaustive week. I went to the hospital to visit you and your dad today. I thought I'd check in with your dad first. He is finally eating again and holding food down, so I've been trying to take advantage of that by meeting his appetite requests. He had a taste for Popeyes chicken. I was quite pleased that I was able to get through the drive-through and out to the hospital in a relatively decent period of time. Traffic was pretty light for a rush hour.

It must have been the Holy Spirit that led me to check on your dad first this time. When I got there, he was a bit nauseous, so he thought he'd ask his nurse for something to help with that. She comes in looking a bit irritated, flinging cords back and forth. Without much of a hello to me, she begins to complain that someone had been playing with the machine all day and that she was very meticulous when she set up the chemo run, and that no one seemed to be admitting they did it, She continued, "I hope they had fun!" Chris, let me tell you, I became so infuriated with that woman! I watched as your dad helplessly looked at me for input. How could she think it was okay to speak so condescendingly to my husband! I stood up and asked her to explain herself. She had no proof that your dad had touched that machine, let alone "played with the cords"!!! Why would he be playing with the cords on the machine for goodness' sake? He's the one taking the stupid chemo!!! Doesn't she realize how hard all this is? I mean, just look at him! He is a mere fraction of himself! Your dad, who was once quite muscular in stature, stood six foot tall and weighed 220 pounds before all this. Now he is feeble and barely weighs slightly more than me! He's been in this hospital bed for several weeks. What in the heck is this woman thinking?

She must have realized that I was obviously upset. She immediately apologized for her tone and confessed that she was out of line. She tried to explain. "It's just that he's pressed the buttons before, and—" And what? I didn't allow her to finish. I told her that was not an excuse to feel that it was appropriate to talk to my husband that way. My mind briefly wondered what you both must endure when I am not around to defend you. I adamantly let her know that we were offended. I didn't want her ridiculous apology. Instead, I insisted that she apologize to my husband! I then told her that just because our family practically lives at this place, they had no right to take our feelings for granted. I mean, my goodness, I have to work! I can't be here with you guys twenty-four hours a day. And I certainly don't want to think that in my absence, your care is diminished in any way. Lord, as if I don't have enough to be concerned about. Just the other day, I had another crazy situation. I got here and your dad's room was not clean. Trash was spewing over from the trash can. You know I can't stand clutter, especially when it comes to germ-infested hospital trash! How is that conducive to healing? I spoke to a supervisor, who was very nice and rectified the situation. Well, at least, while I was there. At that moment, I began to devise a plan to install secret cameras in both your rooms.

So after the obviously unsympathetic apology from this nurse, she offered to have me consult with her manager. I politely declined (as I imagined strangling her) and asked her to never disrespect or be insensitive to my husband again. I then left the room trying to hold back angry tears. She followed me outside, insisting that I should speak one-on-one with her manager. She even directed me to him. Well, you know I don't mean to toot my own horn, but experience has taught me a thing or two. I know the whole "let the customer vent, apologize, and promise to do better bit." Quite frankly, I was infuriated all the more. I told her I didn't have time for this. My time with you and your dad is already limited because of work and other stuff. I refuse to waste valuable time trying to tell people who should be trained how to do their jobs! Don't these people realize, I mean, do they have an ounce of thought that tells them Mrs. Smith is tired? She's the only one working to maintain her house, sanity, and everything else! Can't they see I'm doing all I can just to hold it together and walk a straight line? If only they knew what a chore it is just to get out of bed in the morning, which by the way, I have to do each and every morning because I can't afford to take any time off. I used up all my leave time. I have to go to work and build up more time so we can go to Baltimore for your transplant! Ugh!!! What the heck is wrong with these people?

Baby, I know that they are mere humans. Everyone has a bad day from time to time, I guess. Bad thing about all this is I feel powerless to change it. I wish I could just whisk you both out of here. I wish we were so rich that we could afford the best care that money can buy. So often I question whether I have truly done all that I could do for you and your dad. I mean, maybe I should be more direct. One thing is certain; I am not the do-it-all woman I once thought I was. Each day I carry a proverbial bend on my face—it's this stupid fake smile that says, "Hey, world, I got it all together." I mask my true emotions. Day after day, there is a methodic behavior like a machine. I avoid the subject when someone asks how I feel. I guess, it's another coping mechanism. Otherwise, I know I will fold and become some weakling, probably wind up under some doctor's care myself. Nope, can't let that happen! I mean, I have my moments when I am alone. Even then I'd rather talk to God than allow myself to go off into some depressed state of mind.

You are only back at the hospital this time for pain control. You had been home with me for the weekend after having spent a week with your grandmother. You stayed with her after your last release from the hospital. Then on Sunday night, the bone pain started again. I had selfishly decided we would not be going back to the hospital. It felt so good having you home; that brief sense of normalcy was nice. You were home with me and your brother. I could sleep a little now because you were both home with me! So I took the enemy on and began to pray and speak God's redeeming words over you. But the more I prayed, the more you seemed to be in pain. This confirmed that the enemy was indeed involved in this. After all, you have no trace of cancer in your bloodstream now. According to the oncologist, "Everything looks great!" You insisted on driving yourself to the hospital, especially since your brother was already in bed looking forward to leaving for camp in the morning. I tried to convince you to stay and pray with me. We would pray through the pain together. I reluctantly opened the garage for you as you cranked your car. This scene was all too familiar; it had played out with your dad on several occasions, the most recent being after his return from Indiana.

It's all about the pain. It is my sense that this may be purely psychological. No, I grant you I am not in your shoes. And heaven forbid, I just know what I see and sense as a mother—and as a wife to your dad. Pain is a symptom that occurs as a result of something going wrong in the body. How we react to it will determine how powerful it becomes. I believe the very nature of pain causes you to become fearful so your defense mechanisms are not there. You are then compelled to rely on medicine. That's not necessarily a bad thing; it's just that too much of it may not be the best thing. I believe that all the pain medicine has altered your ability to cope with this! This really bothers me because it can now be a tool for the enemy to prolong this situation. But you know what? God is still in control. You are destined for greatness. My prayer continues to be that you will be encouraged and your mind renewed. I believe God has answered that prayer. You told me yourself that it occurred to you as you drove to the hospital that you should react differently to pain and not let it dictate your state of mind. I believe you can do it!

Yes, I am getting tired. But I am not giving up. This is hard, very hard. It hurts so much that we are going through all this. The anger, frustration, loneliness, restless nights, and the sense of failure. Then trying to maintain everything we have. I could go on and on. But what's the point? This is the stuff people don't see.

Chapter 24

It's Raining on My Side of Town

July 15, 2007

Dear Chris,

People probably think that cancer brings physical pain. It goes much deeper than that. It affects everything and everyone around the patient too. I mean, I feel as though every day is dismal and cloudy. I can't even enjoy the sunshine.

I see others in the sunshine. They are preparing for summer vacations, celebrating birthdays and anniversaries. Some are having picnics in the park, enjoying a movie or weekend meal out. There are even people remodeling their homes. Somewhere someone is celebrating the newfound independence of a child that has graduated from college and started a new life of their own. Oh, how I have longed to be in the sunshine again. To look up at the clear blue sky and breathe in the sweet smell of summer with its hint of jasmine and honeysuckled bushes.

When I look at the sunshine, it is covered by these clouds that seem to follow me everywhere I go. Could the clouds be love? Perhaps they are hovering above me, filtering the sunshine, giving me vital nutrients I need to grow. Nutrients come in the form of people who see me and offer umbrellas of hope and prayer. I can't tell you how often someone walks up to me and hands me some token of love or stops by just to say hello. They tell me they are praying for us. These acts of kindness at times make my heart heavy, but I have come to realize that my heart is not heavy from what may be pity for us—it is overwhelmed with joy. That's not something I'm used to.

I have also learned to appreciate the loneliness in this rain. You see, when I am alone and all is quiet, I can literally hear my heart beat to the sound of God's voice. I can count every beat. I know what it means to meditate and feel His presence. I used to wonder what people meant when they would say God spoke to them. Now I know His voice. It is a calming sense of peace that seems to lead me in the right direction.

These clouds have further caused me to seek God's word for shelter. When I am so lost that I don't know what to do or think, I find myself opening up the Bible more often. I can now read with understanding I had not understood before. It's almost as if God himself is reading His Word to me.

I remember when you and your brother were younger. I used to relish having a few moments to myself to just sit and read a book. I would be content with escaping to the hair salon for a couple of hours to rejuvenate my spirit. Even though the pain of being in this storm and the inconvenience of it all is irritating, I am learning to appreciate the coolness of a dismal gray sky. I walk a little slower. The storm has caused me to slow down, take my time to think before I do things. You know, I've always prided myself on being the great multitasker. A good friend once told me that it is good to be able to do many things, but doing one thing in a great way means so much more. Funny, I really understand that now. By slowing down, I can handle things more definitively with care and precision. In this fast-paced world we live in, it seems it has to take some major event in your life to slow you down and cause you to reflect and become a better person. Of course, I could think of other events I'd rather have slowing me down. But then I can also think of times where God's grace and mercy has saved me from plenty of other events that could have slowed me down as well. So He has allowed this to occur and chosen us for such a time as this. That's another one that I've heard all my life that I now truly understand.

We have two years and counting beyond your doctor's initial expectations. I don't want these letters to ever end. You are my joy and my inspiration; may God continue to bless you, my dear Chris!

Chapter 25

Thanks for Letting Me Vent

July 23, 2007

Dear Chris,

Y ou know what tomorrow is? That's right, another birthday for Mommy! Honestly, I haven't really given much thought to it. There was once a time when I'd make a big deal about celebrating. Over the years, I would look forward to it with great anticipation only for it to arrive and be met with disappointment. Most of the time, I'd find myself frustrated because either the plans I had made wouldn't go as I had hoped or I didn't get what I wanted, typical. So this year I have made up my mind: less expectations mean less disappointment. But despite my attempts to crush any opportunity for failure, I find myself frolicking in irritation with your dad. His mother, your dear sweet grandmother, has been coming to the house daily taking care of him. So after I'd gotten home from a long day at work, he casually mentions to me that she had asked him what I would like for my birthday. The man actually said he had no clue, absolutely no idea. Well, we have only spent the last twenty-plus years of our lives together. Since we moved into the new house, I must have mentioned house plants at least a few times. And what about all this purple and green decor all over the place? I could go on and on about how obvious it was by the dark circles around my eyes that I could use some rest and relaxation—I mean, just look at my hair and nails. Perhaps a salon visit, maybe a day of pampering would be nice. I could go on and on, but really, I am just in a quandary as to why no one seems to know me very well. And it's not just at my birthday, but Mother's Day and Christmas too! Ekkk!

I suppose that I should just be grateful that my birthday is even recognized at all. Perhaps it would be better if it weren't especially if I am not worthy of a sincere gift. So anyway, your dad goes on to tell me that his mom suggested a toaster. A freakin' toaster! Come on, first of all, I have two. One of which I received from your aunt this past Christmas; the other your grandmother previously gave me herself. Hello, she's already given me a toaster. When your dad and I were first married, we had several discussions about toasters—I must have told him a million times that I do not like them.

So our discussion over my birthday and toasters became somewhat heated, and your dad is now saying he never knows what I want. This little statement all but made me snap! You were so sweet to listen to me tonight and let me go on and on about my birthday debacle with your dad. Thank you for letting me vent about it.

As long as I'm venting, there's the bone marrow transplant process, and this whole cancer mess. Period! Things seem to be spiraling out of control. I am being pulled in too many different directions. I am needed to be in this place and that place—I wish I could clone myself. You and your dad have such individual situations, and you both need me so much.

And of course, there's your brother Josh. He is trying so hard to be mature about things. Up until this past week, he was really enjoying being away for the summer at Camp Lake Allatoona. It was a great getaway for him. He even met a girl who he has been talking to on the phone. I'd miss him so much, especially at night, because I would be at home all by myself. But the loneliness was worth it if it meant he was somewhere, smiling and being a kid. According to your brother, the little drama king, this past week, a pack of wild coyotes invaded their camp and scared everyone so much that he refuses to ever go back. He has such a creative imagination! He told me this elaborate story about how their group was having a bonfire, and everyone scattered in all directions when the "coyotes sneaked into the camp." He "hid in a bathroom stall for what seemed like hours." I know, too funny, right?

Chapter 26

Time for Another Season to Change

August 16, 2007

Dear Chris,

Well, another summer is coming to an end; school has started again, and here we are, another hospital stay and another conference with your doctor. He has consulted with the bone marrow physicians, and they think the leukemia is back; this time in your skin. This is based on a pathologist's report from biopsying one of the red bumps that have appeared on your chest and legs. They don't have the official results but are making recommendations about chemo treatment or possibly hospice care. My Lord, I never imagined being at a point of losing count on how many times we've had remission, how many times we've discussed long-term care.

As I sat in traffic on my way to the hospital this morning, my mind drifted and wondered, *Lord, how many times have I driven back and forth out here?* Again they play "Step Aside" on the radio. So I wonder what would happen if I truly trusted God? You know, like they say in another song that seems to speak to me—"Yesterday." So I decided right then and there and just told God, "Lord, I am stepping aside to let you work. You know what is in our hearts and what our desires are. So I have stopped begging and pleading and am just waiting to receive as I praise and thank You for what You have already done."

I don't know if I'll ever fully understand this journey of our lives. Despite whatever we're going through, God continues to give us another day and another moment and another breath. So if He wanted life to come to an end for you and your dad, He could have very well chosen to take you at anytime. He must have a plan. He is using us for some great purpose, and I am honored to be chosen to be so blessed and highly favored that He would even take the time to choose me and my family to be a part of His awesome plan. Oh yes, the load does get heavy sometimes, but praise God for another season and another reason to hope.

Chapter 27

Give It to God

August 20, 2007

Dear Chris,

As I drove away from the hospital today in a tired, almost drunkenlike stupor, I let my voice proclaim, "It's yours, Lord, and I can't do this all by myself!" I had uttered these words several times before. I had spent the night with you in the hospital and spent the morning taking a blood-typing test to be a possible match for your transplant and then meeting with palliative care for your dad while watching him vomit repeatedly. So I just sat in my car for about an hour debating with myself over whether or not to go to work. Part of the great debate was due to the fact that my clothes were wrinkled, and I knew I looked an absolute mess after having spent the night at the hospital. I needed to work this out—*shopping!* That's what I needed to do, go shopping. I figured I'd treat myself to a decent top and shoes to wear to work. It would be a quick inexpensive excursion—a simple pleasurable distraction intended to allow me to blow off some steam. This little retreat of a much-needed mental break culminated into lunch with a gigantic burger and bucket of fries. This would become the first of a guilty-pleasure-turned-habit that would lead to the need-for-a-lot-of-work-to-remove-guilty-pounds-of-ridiculous-pleasure fat! I guess, I got too much pleasure out of this little mental break. I later found myself at the salon for an impromptu hair shampoo and pedicure. As I sat under the dryer enjoying this emotional indulgence, I perused a few magazines and came upon an article on Nancy Wilson, the self-proclaimed song stylist. I have long been drawn to the wisdom of elders. To be of age, surely, they must have gone through some life-altering challenges, and therefore, some wisdom must be theirs to share. The article offered the motto that Ms. Wilson has lived by: "Let go and give it to God; you can't let stress get you down. There's nothing you can do about it anyway." These have been words Ms. Wilson has held on to for nearly seventy years! As I focused in on these words, a conversation was going on next to me among some other salon patrons, and I heard of them say, "Let it go, honey chile. Let God!" Could this be a confirmation? I believe God heard me, and now I truly surrender.

After this day, I can't say I stopped worrying, but I did stop trying to come up with all the answers. I stopped trying to place myself everywhere being everything for everybody. I guess I realized that it was not possible for me to go on with this "superwoman" mentality. I drift in and out of all these different situations never allowing myself time to switch gears. I am not an extraordinary being; God is. Only He can be everywhere all the time and be completely in control.

And when we cross that river—to study war no more
We will sing our song to Jesus, the one whom we adore.

Chapter 28

Grateful

August 12, 2007

Dear Chris,

You know I am always referencing some song to describe my feelings. I suppose that is because music is so much a part of me. Do you remember the song "Grateful"? It says, "Lord, I am grateful, and I praise you for everything you have done for me." That is a powerful sentiment. When you really stop to think of *everything* He has done. Is it even possible to know everything our Lord has done? Let's see. We are taught that He gave the ultimate sacrifice, His only begotten son; He wakes us up each day and starts us on our way, protects us from dangers seen and unseen. But that's not everything. I would venture to say we can't grasp it all; we must be grateful and praise Him without ceasing because He must truly love us so much.

Tomorrow you will start the stem cell process. Finally, we made it to transplant! Yes, I have been quite agitated about the setbacks that almost eluded us from seeing this day—pain, hospitalizations, and infections. I know I was being selfish expecting you to forge ahead despite all these circumstances. I am just so anxious for us to move on with our lives. You have been through so much, and your constant stoic, cynical disposition makes it difficult for those around you to truly understand how you are really feeling. I see your attitude as the way you've chosen to handle the physical, emotional, and mental aspects of all this. I shouldn't complain—who could really? After all, being on the outside looking in can hardly compare to actually being in your shoes.

I know this particular time of the year is particularly difficult for you. Another school year is beginning, and you see your brother in all his excitement about going to the seventh grade. Then there are your friends who are returning, as well as a whole new class of students entering your school. My heart weighs so heavily for you. I sincerely pray that you hold on to your hopes and dreams. Unfortunately, there are challenges ahead for all of us. Everyone has some kind of cross to bear. Hopefully, your struggle can be a light of encouragement for your classmates as they see how determined you are to return to your studies.

Your dad gave us a bit of a scare last night when he became short of breath, and we had him rushed to the emergency room. He and I were so proud of you and Josh the way you reacted and stepped in to lend your support. I was only a bit scared for a moment at the thought of losing your dad. But when he began gasping for air and sweating profusely, there was no time to be afraid; my only focus was survival and our future. It was so good to have you both at home. We were all together again, and as usual, under some great cause of panic, you are the one with the cooler head. You told us all to stay calm and made sure Josh was comforted and not afraid. You even gave me that look that ultimately makes me laugh when you think your dad is being ridiculous. Praise God! A trip to the emergency room by ambulance resulted in a false alarm. It made me realize that while we continue to hold on to our faith, we need to be wise in making sure our affairs are in order. God forbid if things had taken a turn for the worse; I would not have been prepared at all.

Chapter 29

Specific Prayer

August 14, 2007

Dear Chris,

P lease stand firm and know that God is with you. He could have easily taken your dad last night or any time. But again He spared him. God wants us to stay focused, constantly seeking Him. Let's stay strong together.

It is the middle of August. You were readmitted to the hospital yesterday after we started the stem cell collection. It is so hard to watch you in all this pain—it's frustrating; I mean, with all the pain meds you are taking, why aren't they working? It simply isn't logical that someone can take so much pain medicine and not have any relief. The doctors say you are taking enough medicine to take down an elephant. The whole matter of pain simply baffles me, with regard to your dad as well. Since he has been on that pain pump for the past several weeks, the very essence of him seems nonexistent.

I am not believing nor receiving the news we got today about the leukemia coming back. The doctors are being premature and incorrect in their assumptions. We are on our way to transplant! How can this be happening? I mean, how can they make a diagnosis based on a bump on your chest? It is possible their biopsy results are wrong. You've had those bumps before, and it was just a staph infection. Lord! Every time you go into that hospital, they come up with something else.

I know that prayer should be specific. I don't know how much more specific I can be. I have asked God to bring you and your dad home. He did, and I became even more tired with running back and forth with work, more household chores, errands, and doctor visits. I asked God to give me rest and renew my strength. He did, and I was able to relax more as your father's body adapted to involuntarily nausea spells, and I watched in awe as he would clean up after himself and continues to eat anyway. You also began to fend for yourself. You developed insomnia and started taking your meds on your own, keeping up with the dosages and timing yourself. This was somewhat of a relief because some nights, I can actually catch a bit of sleep. I have prayed for and tried to act like everything was back to normal. But what is normal? All of us at home in separate rooms watching the same TV channel? What does this all mean? How specific do I need to be?

Guess, I should stop wondering about the specifics—here we go again. You are back in the hospital contemplating more chemotherapy. Your dad is home taking care of himself, trying not to get in my way as he too contemplates more chemotherapy. I am still so angry and frustrated despite my blessings and all that God has done for me. I wish you could have started the transplant process months ago. They dropped the ball while taking weeks to complete paperwork! Then when they finally approved everything, you had pain issues that delayed the process. Oh yes, and then the doctors went on vacation. Yes, it's summertime, so they take time off, and no one is left to make any real decisions. The on-call doctors are only able to prescribe more pain medicine. I mean, is this really an emergency situation?

I started writing this letter to encourage you and to make you read something other than your cell phone messages while you recover (just kidding). I wanted you to see my life in all of this. At times, I would think about keeping it to myself, then, I began to consider sharing it with others. Looking back over it all, it seems to be a lot of pages of my own heartache and complaints. I wonder who would really want to read this. It is kind of depressing. But I most definitely am not asking for nor should I expect sympathy. I certainly am not one to wallow in some pity party. Could it be possible that this whole experience was meant to bless someone else? I don't want this letter to end. It is our life that starts over every day. I love you so much. I praise God for you and your dad.

Chapter 30

God Next

August 24, 2007

Dear Chris,

We are nearing the end of August. Under the circumstances, I would normally be compelled to ask, what next? In the matter of a week, your dad almost died, and they think you may be paralyzed. I rushed from work to get to you after the doctor shared this news. Okay, I admit it; "superwoman" shed some tears. I began to think about seeing you again. Then I figured we would just lie together in your bed at the hospital and cry in each other's arms for a while. You have been so brave. I know you have needed me. You have wanted and needed my undivided attention, but other circumstances have pulled me away from you. Could it be God is calling for our individual, undivided attention? I believe this to be so. He wants us to completely trust Him.

As I entered the hospital today, I figured that you would be down in radiation therapy. I guess, we will be talking to the lead radiologist again. She has been one of my favorite doctors. She is so caring and compassionate. She even gave me her cell phone number! Of course, I respect her and would never abuse the privilege of being able to reach her directly. I decided to go ahead and get some dinner, figured it would be a long night. My plans to cry all night were foiled! As I approached you, your godfather Sam was already at your side. Wow, that guy really and truly cares for you. Despite his own family and life concerns, he gives so much of himself for us. Anyway, I couldn't find the tears that were previously waiting on standby. While we waited for you, Sam cheered me up. I am not sure if he did that on purpose, but before I knew it, I caught myself smiling again as we exchanged our usual comments about how stubborn and demanding you can be. Now what am I supposed to do with all the tears I was saving up for tonight? This man has me laughing when I just want to cry. Sam is truly god-sent. He has been here for you in the midst of all of this. It is comforting to know that someone else cares so much and can be with you when I can't.

So now as I sit here in this room and watch you sleep, finally allowing yourself to rest. I just trust God. I don't know how much longer this ordeal will continue; it's been two years—so what's next? Only God knows.

I often wonder about the way you are really handling all of this. I want to believe that you have submitted your will to Him and opened up your heart and mind to let God in. I am frustrated at your rebellion when it comes to taking your meds and getting rest. Your dad says that your rebellion is your attempt to have some control, some semblance of the normalcy of a twenty-year-old. Well, I know that your mind can take you places, and when you don't allow the good things of God to come in, then you leave your mind open to other things.

I believe God is working in your life for a purpose. I wish that He would reveal His plan to you, just send an angel to say, "Okay, Chris, enough is enough. Surrender so I can give you all the desires of your heart. Let yourself go. Let your pride go. Forget your anger, fears, frustration, hurts of the past, uncertainty, doubt—let it go and know that I am God."

What's next? God is. You will walk again. We will get through this. God has the last say-so. I don't know exactly why all this has happened; it must be for God's greater good. I continue to see it as a blessing to be chosen for His work. I know that others are watching us to see how we are handling this situation. Despite all that we have been through, God continues to watch over us and protect us. You are going to be just fine. God is still on the throne. Sometimes He allows us to go through changes to change who we are. I do not believe that we have given in. We are not being conformed but rather transformed by this experience.

Chapter 31

Food Fight

August 27, 2007

Dear Chris,

So I'm on my way to work this morning when the phone rings; it's your doctor. It seems that he and the rest of the team of doctors on your case have concluded that you have a tumor on your spinal cord. He said it's inoperable and has paralyzed you from the waist down. They first informed me about this over the weekend, late Friday, I think. And as I write this, I am somewhat hesitant because I certainly don't want to give life or energy to something so . . . Wow, I can't even find the words!

Oh, Chris, if only you knew how much I am struggling with all of this. I love you so much, and as I have said to you before, not being able to simply kiss you and make all of this go away, not having that magical "Mommy hug" to give you comfort, not having any control, it's so hard!

After listening to your doctor use his "stern voice"—that's what he does when he *really* wants me to take him seriously. He went on to say in so many words that they've done all that they can do, and the chemo is being discontinued. "It would be unethical to continue with it," he said. You are no longer a candidate for chemo because you are immobile. And radiation probably isn't going to make much of a difference. Sweetie, he then raised his voice and yelled at me. "You need to stop all this pushing and honor his wishes," he finally said.

I admit I have been pushing, insisting that they try this and that—anything that may have a remote possibility of making you better. It's not easy to accept that someone you love so much may be slipping away. I don't want to give up; we have to exhaust all options! But somewhere in the midst of my thoughts, all the words from the doctor kind of came and went through my ears. So I put on my famous game face; you know, the one where I smile and not make eye contact with anyone. I actually caught some kind of stuffy nose, and this stupid cold medicine has my head all crazy so I'm out of sorts. I was running late again, so I didn't have time to comb my hair. And yes, I'm way overdue for a perm! So I showed up at an event today looking and feeling bloated with spongy hair, basically like crap. Yes, another one of my fabulous ceremonies for one of our projects at work. I actually do just about all the planning and logistics for these things; I have to be there to make sure everything works out according to plan. So I had a lot going on when your doctor called. I didn't take in what he said; I simply didn't have time. You and I spoke earlier, and I know you expected me to drop everything and come to the hospital. But you must remember that a superwoman, a real Renaissance woman does it all! I have to plan my days accordingly. You see, despite illness and all that comes with it, life goes on and so do the bills. Mama's gotta work!

I hurried through the event so I could get to the hospital to be with you. Your grandma Althea was with you when I got there. She said you had just come out of radiation therapy. A few minutes later, the Kaiser coordinator was outside your door motioning for me to come outside. Your doctor had written orders for inpatient hospice care for you. Again, words began to just float in and out as she rambled out names of organizations as if I understood all this. Lord, how do I make a decision about the rest of your life in a matter of minutes? So I asked her to give me the information on all the facilities. No time was wasted. Within the hour, there was a representative at the hospital from each place to talk to me. It's funny being on the outside of health care; you never know if you're getting the full picture of everything. You wonder if you are being given all the best options or if they are merely working to meet their own objectives. I mean, how do you really know? You don't; you just have to pray and trust that the best options are truly there for you, unless you have the means to do otherwise and search for more.

As each representative talked to us, you, being the consummate gentleman, listened intently and thanked them for their time. You said, "I'm not worried." You went on to say that you were trusting God, and what I had surmised as careful planning and preparation, in your opinion, was sending a message to God that we weren't willing to wait on Him. In short order, you began to get agitated with me, telling me I was getting on your nerves. We have such a communication problem. That's why I'm writing these letters to you. You seem to take all my words, all my efforts, and confuse them so much that most of the time, I don't even know what I'm doing! For example, and I know you would think I'm way off base here, you have been having digestive problems, yet you continue to eat all kinds of junk like burgers and fries. You won't eat any vegetables, anything that will help with your digestion. I asked you to eat some green beans; you ignored me until I literally begged you to try. Then I watched as you used your weak hands to finally shove some in your mouth. You became more agitated when I tried to help you, yelling at me, "I told you I didn't want any!" Yes, I know it's all quite trivial now. I had to catch myself from snapping back at you as I have done so often in the past. With all I am going through, it's hard to be an emotional punching bag today. Soon after, the nurses were there to clean and take care of you. I quietly excused myself to leave to pick up your brother.

Dear Chris

Prior to our little "bean spat," we actually did have a few minutes to talk. You said you didn't want to do hospice care. You wanted to come home. You were perfectly fine with me taking care of you. You and everyone seems to need me, but I can't dedicate myself to any one area full time. I know if you come home this way, it will be too much for me to manage. I don't know if I'm getting weaker or if I'm just tired. It pains me to see you going through so much; all we can truly do is trust God.

Chapter 32

Hope Changes

August 28, 2007

Dear Chris,

In all my life, or at least as far back as I can remember, I have known the phrase "hope never fails." Well, today when I found myself at a weak point, one of the nurses told me you don't lose hope; sometimes your hope just changes. These words of encouragement came after she had come by to check on you. So many of the nurses have come to know and adore you. They stop by even at times when you are not a part of their rounds. They feel you are a part of the family. So many people are affected by or, should I say, infected by you! You seem to have this effect on people that draws them to want to be close to you. Despite all this talk of hospice, the paralysis, the progression of this awful disease, I'd held back tears until this one nurse came in today, and away went the floodgates. It's as if I began to feel the finality of it all. She hugged me and went on her way. I'd tried to go back to straightening your room, and you called me over and held me. Again the tears just flowed. You offered me water and made me promise not to have any more emotional outbreaks. You told me to stay strong and trust God because you were at peace with all of this.

Earlier during our visit today, you said you decided to do inpatient hospice because you didn't want yourself or your family dealing with any additional stress. I can certainly understand your decision. As I watch you struggle to feed yourself and the nurses helping you to do even the simplest things that you can no longer do for yourself, baby, it's hard. And, yes, I want you home with us. I want to take care of you. But I know that I still couldn't be there for you the way you need me to be. I plan to go and visit the hospice centers tomorrow to get a sense of how they operate. I need to be comfortable with where you are. It's funny you said you envision those places as being like "people walking around in straight jackets." You can make me laugh even in the midst of all this. Yet I too do not really know what to expect. Each hospice representative explained that the patients there are primarily elderly and "in their final stages." Lord, I can't do this! I am asking God for a miracle. I simply cannot even begin to imagine you off in some strange place, just waiting, with no one to talk to, no recreation to keep your mind active, just off somewhere taking pain medicine to "keep you comfortable." Chris, I can't do this; I'm not ready.

On the way home after picking up your brother, I told him about the paralysis in your legs. He was devastated and came into the house very upset. Your dad then became upset because he thought we should have been together as a family when we told him. This further upset me, and then I broke my promise. I had promised myself that no matter what, I would no longer argue with your dad. He needs his strength to get better. But an argument ensued. He just really knows how to push my buttons! I found myself tempted to toss your father over the deck! That's right; I can lift him now. We've since calmed down, of course. This is all truly taking a toll. I suppose you would probably be upset with me too for telling Josh. But your brother asked me once to be straight with him, and I promised that I would. While I know that I can't always "keep it real," I do think that it's important that he knows what is happening. He took this pretty hard, and we are praying because he is so angry, and he doesn't know who to be angry at. He recognizes that he needs to channel this anger. He told me that he felt like hitting someone or something. He said he's tired of going to school every day and acting as if everything is normal. Lord knows I understand. It's all I can do to hold my head up when I go to work. There have been times when I just felt like yelling at work; these words pound against my brain to be released from thought: "Don't you people realize that I'm tired! I spent the night in the emergency room." or "How in the heck do I keep up with all the medicines and doctors' instructions, provide emotional support at home, and come in here to work with you people!" But for the most part, these thoughts are calmed by the empathy of my coworkers. I believe they can read my face and tell that all is not well. They try not to ask too much of me. I have been quite blessed with some pretty cool coworkers. Some just stop by my office to say hello and offer prayers for us. I know I must look a hot mess too. My hair really needs some help. I've gained a ton of weight—those late-night brownie bites (but thank God for chocolate, only God could create something so enticingly wonderful). Can you believe, for the first time in nearly twenty years, my face is breaking out? What's the deal? I know, minor ridiculous, petty complaints. I can still be cute and fat. In the right clothes, I can make size 12 work! Okay, so maybe some people don't consider size 12 to be "fat," but going from my usual size 7/8, it's a bit awkward for me . . . Um, yeah, I am kind of plump right now.

Sweetie, I will continue to trust God. I am not quite sure about this new "hope changes" school of thought. But I suppose it makes sense. Your dad started driving again today. He surprised us all by showing up at the hospital. My hopes for him and you remain toward healing—complete healing. I can also hope that God gives us all the strength and courage to accept whatever His will is. If He has plans beyond healing, my hope is that both you and your dad will remain in His peace and never-ending love and mercy.

Chapter 33

Another Day

August 29, 2007

Dear Chris,

Praise God for yet another day. It's Wednesday morning, and your dad and I are here at the hospital with you. He insisted on coming with me. We hurried to get your brother off to school so we could be with you. You called me around five thirty this morning to say that your left arm was getting weaker. I tried to comfort you in the only way I knew how—through prayer and reinforcing positive words, finally telling you not to give up on God. You then said I had given up on you because I wasn't there. Baby, I would never give up on you! We stayed with you all day today. Your grandma Althea was here too.

When you went down for radiation therapy, we decided to go visit one of the hospice centers. It was actually nice. As the greeter took us on the tour, I was overtaken by tears—they seemed to just come all of a sudden out of nowhere. The place had these beautiful gardens, a view of the city's skyline. The greeter explained that you would have your own private room. The rooms are set up like cottages. The decor throughout the facility reminded me of the antebellum age. As we left, I wondered if you would really like it there. Your dad didn't feel we should make any hasty decisions because we are trusting that God will give us a miracle. When we got back to your hospital room, it wasn't like we planned it, but we each started rubbing your legs and feet and telling you that we believed you would walk again. We were also pleasantly surprised to find our dear friend and youth pastor there visiting with you. We had seen him earlier this morning on our way to the hospital. Every believer should be so blessed to have a pastor they also call friend, someone who is there in their time of need. We had a nice visit with him, sharing a conversation about you and your brother Josh. He prayed with us. He is leaving to visit his parents in Chicago, who are celebrating their sixtieth wedding anniversary! Wow, that's pretty amazing—I wonder if your dad and I could put up with each other that long. What a blessing!

Dear Chris

There may be hope yet, we've got seventeen years in so far—well, twenty-one, if you count all that dating and trying-to-find-ourselves stuff. That's a lifetime itself. You know, I praise and thank God for your dad. Without him, I would never have met you! Praise God for you!

Glory Hallelujah—You are the reason why I sing
Glory Hallelujah—I give the praises to you
Glory Hallelujah—You are the reason why I sing

Chapter 34

Jeremiah 29:11

August 31, 2007

Dear Chris,

Ⅰt is midnight, and we are all here at the hospital with you. Around 9:00 p.m., you began to have increased breathing problems. They had been running tests all day to determine why you were short of breath. It had started earlier in the day. I wrestled with whether I should go into the office or come to the hospital. For the past few days, you have been telling me that you miss me. Yesterday, you asked when you could have me all to yourself. I promised to come back; my dad even called me to say that Josh could come over to their house for the weekend. So I looked forward to telling you that we would spend the weekend together.

I finally left the office around three thirty and stopped to grab us some dinner and, of course, Fruity Pebbles. That's all you have wanted to eat for the past few days, nothing else! You scoff at my every attempt to ease in a vegetable here and there. Your granddad William and grandma Betty picked Josh up from the after-school program. I figured if Josh asked you to eat with him, you would; my usual trickery didn't really work, but you did let me give you two green beans and a bite of meatloaf with potatoes. I had to pout and insist, and you reluctantly ate. I don't understand what is happening! You are now complaining about chest pain and beginning to struggle to breathe. After you ate, you were fine. I am sending Josh out of the room with grandma Althea. I need to start making phone calls. I want to snatch your phone! Who could you possibly be texting right now while you are struggling to breathe? The doctor explained that if you began to have trouble breathing, they could put you on a respirator (intubate). But you were clear that you didn't want to be on a machine and that you did not want to be resuscitated. I don't think you know the magnitude of that decision. Your grandma Althea has been at the hospital with you all day today. She's been here every day recently. Earlier, you asked us both how we felt about your decision. While we both agreed that we would want you to be resuscitated, you then said, "Grandma, you have to understand. Sometimes you get tired of being sick and tired."

For the past few days, a little over a week or so, it has been quite a ride. You came to the hospital for pain, then your legs started getting weak. They found a tumor on your spine, and then you were paralyzed and unable to use or control your body functions. Then a couple of days later, you called me to say that your left arm and hand had grown weak. And now, here we all are watching over you.

The doctor is telling us that all the tests they have done throughout the day came back normal. There was no blood clot, no pneumonia, your body is failing, and she figures that you will likely pass away in the night. They have offered to keep you comfortable so you wouldn't feel any pain. As they begin to administer these medicines, I cling to your every word as you tell me that you love me and ask me to remain calm. You are saying everything will be all right.

One of our pastors visited you earlier today. Your grandma Althea told me that you were doing fine, laughing and talking during her visit, but as soon as she left the room, you started complaining about chest pain, and they had to put you on oxygen. Your grandma thought you were having some kind of anxiety attack because you didn't want the pastor to leave. I jokingly asked if the pastor had taken the anointing with her. She was kind enough to come back to the hospital tonight when I called. She stayed and prayed with us. She talked to your brother about what was happening. When I sent him out earlier, I couldn't bring myself to tell him what was happening. Your dad is here now; against my concern for his safety, he drove himself to the hospital. He doesn't want to tell Josh either. The pastor made us realize that Josh needs to know and that he needs to see you for what may be the last time. We brought Josh back in; he held your hand and cried as he tried to talk to you.

Several prayers have been offered over you. Our senior pastor even came, and we had prayer. My parents' pastor came and prayed too. It's funny; he touched your arm, and you kind of opened your eyes. I wonder if his spirit touched yours. Throughout his prayer, I could tell you were trying to wake up as if you wanted to say something.

We finally sent Josh home with my parents, with foolish hopes that he will be able to sleep and go to school the next day. He was so upset. Praise God for your godfather Sam. He took Josh in his arms and talked to him. I don't know what he said, but whatever it was, it worked. Josh calmed down. He was still tearful when he left but a bit more at ease. He loves you so much. You have played a major role in his life, helping to mold him and shape the personality of the strong man that I know he will become.

Everyone here with you tonight loves you so much. Sam is and always has been such a blessing. I ask him all the time if he is getting enough rest. I don't know how I could have gotten through this without him. He said from the start that he was in this for the long haul. He has been here with you every day, often spending the entire night. It really is true that God puts people in our lives for a reason. Sometimes it is only for a season. You can usually tell which ones are meant to stay and which ones are meant to come and go. Sam is definitely a keeper! When it became apparent that you and your dad were battling these cancers for an undetermined amount of time, Sam stepped right in. He made sure you were taken care of and stayed by your side.

As I watch you now sleeping, I wonder if you are really and truly just resting. The doctor had come by earlier and told your brother that you were halfway to heaven. I thought of one of my favorite songs by Kenny G and Céline Dion, "Halfway to Heaven." You downloaded it for me as a gift along with several of your other favorite tunes. Should the Lord call you to come home tonight, I will have this music played at your services. Wow! I can't believe I actually just wrote that. Honestly, it has been on the back of my mind. I have had some revelations, and I now know they were to prepare me. Yet I yield to what is human, and I continue to pray otherwise. Now I am thinking about your call the other morning when you said that I wasn't with you, that I had given up on you. As I watch them continually giving you pain medicine, I can't help but wonder if this is me giving up on you. No, baby, I never gave up on you, but I have decided to give you up to God. It's the only way you can be free. You have served your purpose here, and now God is calling His sweet angel home. I truly believe that when a child goes to be with the Lord, He must have been sent as an angel in disguise to live among us and bring us closer to God. After all, aren't children the closest to heaven anyway?

Punkin, I have held on to you so tightly since the moment we first met. I have always tried to make my own plans for you. I am a planner. Each day was mapped out. It started at preschool and continued through college. I would plan to meet your teachers, decide which activities were best for you, all with the ultimate purpose of preparing you for manhood. But the funny thing about plans is that they never seem to work out exactly as they are drawn. It's like you plan to wear a particular outfit, and then your hair decides to go its own way so you have to style it differently. This further means that now you have to change your outfit. And for me, this can alter my entire day. Sometimes our plans do work out, I suppose. But most often, life just happens, and you plan around it.

God's word tells us that He is the great planner. You may recall when you were initially diagnosed, I was in the hospital cafeteria with our cousin Pam talking about more of *my* plans for you. This woman who appeared to work at the hospital just seemed to show up out of nowhere and gave me a piece of paper with Jeremiah 29:11 written on it. She didn't say anything. She just laid the paper on the table and quickly walked away. I read the paper and looked up, and she had disappeared. I thought, How weird is that? Some crazy person leaving paper on the table. Was that an angel? Was God telling me to stop all *my* plans and let Him work? Well, I didn't understand it then, but for a long time, I tried to figure it out. I read the scripture over and over: "For I know the plans I have for you, to prosper and not harm you." What did those words mean? I do not fully understand, but I am beginning to. I suppose they could mean a lot depending on how you read and receive them. When the scripture was given to me, I wasn't ready to receive it. Now I am trusting that God really does know the plans He has for us. I am not clear on the prosperity in all this though; perhaps you are on your way to being prosperous in the happiness of a time and place of being with Him forever.

I want to keep writing, but this letter is coming to end. You always let me know that you loved me. I will love you forever. The mere thought of being without you feels as though my heart is being ripped out. I would never want to be so selfish that I would just sit by and watch you suffer. I know you would want to live a better life, and if keeping you here with me means watching you suffer daily, then that is not the existence that should be for either of us. I would rather you be at peace with no more pain.

I praise God for you. His plans for you to be a part of my life for this brief period of time were just that—His plans. While I would have my own ideas, I am now willing to let go. I love you too much for otherwise. Rest now, my son. Don't worry because God knows the plans He has for me.

I sing because I'm happy, I sing because I'm free
His eye is on the sparrow, and that's the reason why I sing.

CONCLUSION

Chapter 35

Gone but Forever You Live in My Heart

October 28, 2007

Dear Chris,

I t has been almost two months since you left me. A couple of days after you passed away, I was doing everything I could to feel you. I stared at the pearl necklace you gave me for my birthday (you were so sweet after hearing me complain about sincere gifts). I lay in your room and wrapped myself in your clothes. I searched my phone for your text messages and came upon one I had not opened. It was dated the day you passed away. I remembered my agitation with you because you were using your energy to send text messages. I now realize that in those hours after midnight, when in frustration I wondered who you're texting, it was me. Your message read, "It's gonna be all right"; it was your last message.

I am thanking God because He allowed you to visit me a few nights ago. After you passed away, I was even more saddened because I could not find you in my dreams. Each night, I went to bed eager with anticipation in hopes of seeing you. I thought, surely you would come to me to let me know you were okay, but nothing. Then there was this night; it was wonderfully amazing! We were sitting together in a restaurant having lunch. We talked about Josh and your dad. We were both laughing so hard! You always did make me laugh. We were leaving the restaurant and heading down a stairway; it was dimly lit. It was like a basement with cement walls. You kept hugging me and smiling. I could literally feel your arms around me. I really miss your hugs. You always made me feel so safe and loved. Although I was enjoying our time together, I began to cry. Somehow I knew I was dreaming, but I wasn't fully asleep. I looked up at you and asked the Lord to forgive me because I didn't know if I should tell you that I knew this was just a dream. I sobbed as I uttered these words to you, "Baby, you died on August 31." You then looked down at me as if to say you were in on this surprise visit. You gently pulled away from me and began to sway as if you were growing weak, just like you did at the hospital before you died. You fell into my arms, and we both fell against the wall. Then there were other people walking quickly past us. As I sat there holding your body with my tears streaming down, you began to dissolve away. When I woke up, I just lay there feeling overjoyed, bewildered, and amazed. I must have awakened your dad. He rose up and asked me if I was okay. I told him every detail of the dream. For the first time, I had such a strong sense of peace, like you were telling me that you were happy.

You have visited me in other ways that I now understand. After you passed away, I could still feel your presence in your bedroom. Often in the middle of the night, we could hear sounds in your room as if you were messing around in your closet. One night, we finally stopped acting as if we individually were hearing these sounds. We looked at each other, and your dad asked me, "Do you hear that?" I replied yes. When you were alive, you would drive us bananas messing around in your closet late at night. I can recall us yelling at you to go to bed. Your closet is right next to our room, so when we would be trying to sleep, your dad would say you were "fumbling" around in there. Your dad and I agreed that we knew some part of you was here in the house. A few nights after that, I went into your closet. It has become a place of refuge for me where I go to talk to you. I found the strength to speak to that part of your spirit that was there and release you. I told you that I was okay and that your brother was okay. I told you that you could go and be at peace because God would look after us now. With that, the room became cold. I haven't heard those noises since.

For the past few days, the sense of peace that I had after my dream has been shaken. Every night, I am again finding it hard to get to bed and rest. I am drenched in despair. I believe you asked God to allow that dream. I had visited your grave site earlier that day. You must have heard my weeping there and felt my broken heart. Tonight is the first time I've written to you since my last letter after you passed away. It's funny; I picked up my pad and found letters that I had written in your last days. I had actually forgotten about them. The letters went from the day that your doctor decided to close your case to the day you told me that you were at peace. I often wonder if you knew you were leaving me. You were so brave, so strong. I still can't believe you are really gone. Your brother will turn thirteen tomorrow. We spent time this weekend looking for new shoes. I wanted his birthday to be special. But I honestly put no effort in making it so. I wish you were here. I feel as if I am slowly falling apart. Not going all out for your brother's birthday is completely out of character for me. I didn't even get a cake. I now just pray that God will keep our family strong.

Chapter 36

The End of Our Journey

April 6, 2008

Dear Chris,

I finally finished writing this letter to you. When I started writing that letter on August 31, 2007, I was sitting in the hospital room with you. I sat there watching you vigorously fight for your life. I would later realize that the body I saw in so much pain was fighting on its own and your spirit had already begun to see the angels. In fact, as I came to what I had planned to be the conclusion to this letter, you went into your highest level of distress. I wondered if you had left your body as if to interrupt my writing to gain my attention. Many times before, you had stared at me as I would write; you knew that my writing was a form of release that helped me put a pen to my true emotions.

That night as your life came to an end, I stopped writing to hold your hand. I began tending to you, wiping the sweat from your brow, and talking to you. And though you could not answer me, somehow I knew you could hear and understand me. Your dad and I had stayed with you throughout the night along with your grandma Althea and aunt Terri. We literally stayed awake all night just staring at you. And then a little after 7:00 a.m. the next morning, your nurse and PCT came in along with the doctors. They administered what would be your last dose of pain medicine. I then asked how much longer you could possibly struggle so hard to breath. You had been under the highest levels of oxygen all night—just hours before, I had begun to get frustrated and yelled at the nurses telling them that you were not getting the oxygen; it wasn't getting into your lungs. I wanted them to do something! But they held steadfast to instructions you had given the previous day, not to put you on any machines to sustain you. So in response to my question of "how long?" one by one, they each said, "Not long." It could be minutes or hours, but not long. Your grandmother and aunt somehow decided to leave the room; I attempted to step away to rest my eyes when suddenly, I heard your father tell me to get up and come quickly. With him on one side of you and me on the other, we watched you as your breathing all of a sudden began to calm down. You were no longer perspiring as you had been all night. The nurse removed the oxygen mask and left the room. I began to feel a sense of joy; I saw you looking so peaceful as if you were drifting into a deep sleep. Then you took your last few breaths; I felt your body wiggle, and then you were gone. It was the most beautiful thing I'd ever seen aside from the day I first met you. It was as if you had asked God to leave you alone with us to say good-bye. Your dad said it was a true full circle of life; we both realized the blessing in being with you when you took your first and last breaths of life. And memories of the breath that had lasted twenty years began to unfold in my mind. I felt such joy and peace at that final moment, and I just began to praise God for you and for allowing us to have such an experience! The next moment, I realized that my sweet joy, my precious little prince was gone. I became weak and began to weep uncontrollably and scream in agony; the life that I had shared for the last twenty years was gone. I lost a part of myself that day.

Praise God for the nurses; they all came out of nowhere and just embraced me. I finally calmed down and rushed back to you; I didn't want to stop kissing your face. I will never forget the look of peace you had, as if you had seen something great and wonderful, something you had been looking forward to that you never imagined you would actually have.

Then it was time to get things in order, and as we gathered your things, I began the hardest process of all, living without you. I continued to try to hold on to you. Your dad and I gathered your things as you lay there at peace. I began the process of making the phone calls to the church, the mortuary, etc. It was all so mechanical. I don't know how I knew what to do. Your dad went to get the car, leaving me with the honor of escorting your body to the hospital morgue. Things seemed to move in slow motion as they covered your head and wheeled you down the corridors of the hospital. I was like stone, my face expressionless and frozen. As I glided along behind you, my mind went from sadness, to anger, to resentment, to blank. My thoughts drifted back to the beginning of all this, when you were wheeled into this hospital on that cold rainy February night. Then thoughts returned to the many times you walked into this place on your own. I thought of the many strolls we had taken together during your admissions there. I wish we had taken the time to stroll through the mall or the park more often when you were well. Where were our true priorities when we had the time? There I was watching as they prepared you for the funeral home. This all seemed so cold as you were loaded like a package through the basement and into a van. I wanted to hold you one more time, baby. I wanted to make sure you were warm enough. But I just stood there and let the driver do his job. He shook my hand and assured me that everything would be taken care of. Then he drove away with you. I stood there even more frozen. There was no one there to hold or comfort me. The halls were empty. Somehow I found my way back to the front of the hospital where your dad was waiting. He was in your car; that's when I recalled that he had driven your car to the hospital. So I followed him home and began the business of planning a beautiful celebration of your life.

I am so thankful for the love and support of our family, your godparents and friends, and our church—all of whom have been with us along this journey and countless others who have come to offer their prayers and support. This experience has truly taught me the meaning of family, the joy of friendships, and the wonder of opening my heart to others.

I am told that time will heal the hurt. Each day begins and ends for me in sweet sorrow, and the hours in between are filled with lackluster emptiness. I am numb. We will never forget this experience, this illness. Despite all that it threw at you, it did not win. You fought the good fight of faith, and your glory became the victor. Praise God you were not left to live a life that was not meant for you. I knew for a while that you were no longer the man that you would have wanted to be.

I had a dream one night, several months before you actually left me. In it, the sky shone with the brightest sun I'd ever seen. I was lost in the midst of a crowd searching for you, pushing my way through, trying to find you. I began to feel a deep sadness. I heard you calling me, and then I felt your hand touch my shoulder. Suddenly, you were there behind me. As I turned around, there you were in all your glory, fully dressed in a fitted tuxedo. Your skin was radiant. Your hair was shiny and wavy, just the way it would be after a fresh haircut. You were smiling that wide beautiful bright smile. You were so handsome, wearing a custom-fitted tuxedo with a crisp white collar and navy striped tie. We held each other. You apologized to me and took my hand, leading me through the crowd. As we walked, the day turned to night, and you led me behind a building to a horse-drawn carriage under a moonlit sky. You literally hopped inside with fervent energy. I watched you change into your white tee and Jordan neck chain. There was a young lady sitting inside as if she was waiting for you. She asked you how long you had been gone. Just as you were putting your earphones in to your MP3 player, you answered, "I've been gone for a while now." You told me you loved me as the carriage pulled away. I called out to you, but there was no answer as the carriage disappeared into the night.

There had been other visions and dreams before that I now understand were God's way of preparing me. No mother wants to say she expects to lose her child, but I haven't lost you. You were a gift, only mine for a while, and God decided to call his sweet angel back home. He has other plans for you. I know I'll see you again.

Chapter 37

Joy and Pain, Like Sunshine and Rain

December 1, 2009

Dear Chris,

It's funny how opposites are similar; how good and bad need each other to define themselves. They say there are several different emotions associated with grief. I have been lonely, helpless, hopeless, angry, anxious, confused, and bewildered. I used to lie in your bed at night, rub my face against your clothes, and stare with searching eyes at your pictures for hours. I still find myself drifting from your closet to your dad's, clinging onto your clothes to fill my nostrils with some remnants of your scents. What does it all mean? Where do I go from here? Do I just say, "Oh well, and let's move on"? I dare say absolutely not! Punkin, this all has to mean something. Perhaps it's something greater than us, even unimaginable. I don't know if I will ever even truly begin to understand.

February 12, 2008, we said our final good-bye to your dad. I woke up the next morning and stared at the ceiling. In a whisper, I confessed to God that I didn't want to go on; I had no joy left in me. Once again, I could literally feel my mind teetering on the line between sanity and insanity. Somewhere in the silence, I heard the words "Jesus is the center of my joy." Could this perhaps be the lesson in all of this? Then I could hear your brother's voice inside my head; he still needs me. I immediately jumped out of bed and began to refocus and rededicate my life to Christ. If losing you and your dad was necessary for Him to get my full attention, then I truly submit. I am paying attention and listening intently for his instructions. I often refer to the story of Job and the blessing of restoration after Job decided to worship God anyway, despite all the pain and loss he endured. I struggled with the notion of imagining true happiness without you both. For so long, my life, my joy has centered around my family. Everything I have done and lived for was for us. All these years, had I idolized my family by living for and serving all of you? Had I placed my heart for my family above my heart for Him?

Dear Chris

As I ponder these thoughts, I realize that my relationship with God is developing into something intimate. I hear His voice; He truly speaks to me, and it's so real.

I am grateful that God brought me through all this.

Since you both went on to your eternal rest, the Lord has been faithful in blessing us. Josh and I are doing well and experiencing blessings at school and at work. I only need to look at Josh, and I can see you and your dad. He has your hands and long legs and your dad's smile. I see both of you in his eyes, and I hear your voices every time he speaks. You would be so proud of him. He maintains an A average at school and is quite a social butterfly. It gets hard for him at times, but he exists as a normal teenager—dare I call that a blessing. He is pursuing his interest in performing arts, focusing on drama and theater.

Perhaps the biggest change in our lives has been the gift of inspirational praise through music. As the days go by, people call me an inspiration. They wonder how I continue to smile. They compliment me and call me an inspiration. Some have said that thoughts of me motivate and inspire them to get through their own challenges. After hearing that, I realized that God has given me a gift to inspire others. One day, I found myself singing again. It had been so long since I uttered a note. I didn't think I would sing again, but praise and worship is what keeps me moving forward. And I want to share that with the world. I am singing professionally now and sharing messages of praise, inspiration, and triumph at every opportunity!

I am committed to honoring your lives by doing all that I can do to make sure your experiences are an example to be learned from. I know you both touched the lives of many doctors and nurses. It is my hope that you not only touched their hearts but their thought processes as well, giving more in-depth meaning to what they do in the lives of others every day. I further hope that your cases can be studied and used to help other cancer patients. I am establishing memorials in both of your honor. I wanted to do something that would be meaningful to each of you. Your dad took pride in helping others, so I am establishing a foundation in his honor that will be committed to assisting low-income families and individuals in need of resources to obtain decent housing and education. You know we struggled for so long to have a nice home, and it will be a blessing to help others to have the same. For you, there is the Dear Chris scholarship fund. This will enable African American males with illnesses and / or disabilities to attend the college of their choice. So I have a lot of work to do!

For months now, I have struggled with publishing these letters. I don't want to let go of so much that I have held so close. But this struggle and all that I have gained and lost is not just for me to keep to myself. I pray that you won't mind me sharing these letters so others will come to know the true power and goodness of our Lord and Savior, Jesus Christ. Perhaps in doing so, they will become inspired to join the fight to find a cure for all forms of cancer and, finally, so that someone will be encouraged to keep their fight of faith, trust God, stay close to family and friends, and bless others.

Dear Chris

The pain of losing you and your dad has not gone away. Almost daily, I go back and forth between joy and sorrow. At times, I find myself drifting away in my thoughts of both of you—moments turn into hours, and I have to catch myself. Almost everywhere I turn, every song I hear, almost anything reminds me of you. I am glad to know and understand that God created nature with a set of laws that allow for rejuvenation. Yes, the pain of loss is there, but with death, there is also rebirth. We have to stay focused for the restoration that God has in store for us. I will never stop believing in the impossible, dreaming beyond imagination, recreating myself, and living for the author of our universe. My destination is the sky.

For now, I say farewell, dear one. I continue to pray for your eternal peace. I know that you and your dad are now among the angels that watch over us by day and night. My heart longs for the day when we are all together again.

Forever in love with you,
Mom

Oh I love you—I love your name Jesus
Glory Hallelujah
For the rest of my life Jesus
You'll be the reason why I sing.

—Kirk Franklin

Let us pray.

Father, we thank You for each and every day.

We ask that You keep us close to You along the way.

Open our eyes and hearts to see what's real and true,

forsaking all others and only trusting You.

Give us the grace to accept the challenges as they come,

for they are meant to make us strong.

The strength that comes from within is where we ultimately find peace,

leaning on to Your arms to rest with You where we belong.

Let the meditation of our hearts and the words our mouths

be acceptable unto You,

our Lord, our strength, and our redeemer.

Amen.

Resources

If you or someone you know is suffering from a long-term illness, seek God's guidance and grace. Have a willing heart to reach out to others as you go through life's storms. There are numerous resources to find out more information about cancer or to seek support. A special appreciation to some of the organizations that helped us along the way:

- American Cancer Society
- American Leukemia Society
- American Red Cross
- Angel Flight
- Cascade United Methodist Church
- National Cancer Institute
- Salvation Army
- Springfield Baptist Church
- Zion Hill Baptist Church

About the Author

Valerie is a rhythm and praise singer/songwriter. She began Inspired by Valerie Music & Entertainment as a result of searching for meaning and purpose in her life. Her personal testimony of sacrifice and surrender can be heard in the expressive tones of a voice that ranges from high alto to second soprano. Valerie's literary works are based upon a foundation created by a lifetime of faith and perseverance.

In 2005, her best friend and oldest son, Christopher, became ill. He battled for two years with cancer before accepting his heavenly invitation to dwell in eternity. Shortly thereafter, her confidant, backbone, supporter, and husband, Elgin, also accepted the hand of Christ after suffering from cancer and joined their son, Christopher.

Valerie desires to share her story as a way of expressing God's love and redeeming power to the world. Her music is designed to motivate and encourage others with the message that a determination to remain focused in the face of adversity will always lead to true purpose and fulfillment as God intends.

Beyond the music, she is working toward establishing memorials for her husband, Elgin, and their son, Christopher. Dear Chris, named in honor of Christopher Jermaine Smith, is a scholarship program that aids African American males with physical disabilities in obtaining their higher educational goals. Proceeds from the book *Dear Chris* will be used to fund this initiative. LeBaron Lights, named in honor of Elgin LeBaron Smith, is a resource company that offers housing and job training assistance to low-income persons.

Valerie currently resides in Atlanta, Georgia, with her youngest son, Joshua, who is also the encouragement behind all her endeavors. She is a member of Cascade United Methodist Church, where she sings with the New Advent Choir, and ministers with the United Methodist Women, Christian Doorkeepers, and Youth Ministry groups.

Get Published, Inc!
Thorofare, NJ 08086
01 April, 2010
BA2010091